Fodor's POCKET 2001

pari

D0716847

fodor's travel publications
new york · toronto · london · sydney · auckland

www.fodors.com

Excerpted from *Fodor's France 2001*

contents

ON THE ROAD WITH FODOR'S

EVERY TRIP IS A SIGNIFICANT TRIP. Acutely aware of that fact, we've pulled out all stops in preparing *Fodor's Pocket Paris*. To guide you in putting together your Paris experience, we've created multiday itineraries and regional tours. And to direct you to the places that are truly worth your time and money, we've rallied the team of endearingly picky know-it-alls we're pleased to call our writers. Having seen all corners of Paris, they're real experts. If you knew them, you'd poll them for tips yourself.

Simon Hewitt headed to Paris straight from studying French and art history at Oxford. He moved to Versailles in 1996 to gain a different perspective on the French capital, and over the years has learned that life does *not* revolve around the capital, contrary to popular Parisian belief. When not contemplating the Sun King's bicep-flexing baroque palace, his thoughts often turn to cricket—he is captain of the French national team. He also writes regularly about antiques and the art market.

Nicola Keegan was born in Ireland and raised in Iowa. But after spending one year at the Sorbonne university, she knew Paris was going to be her home forever. She has now been there 12 years and has become an expert at finding her way around France. In Practical Information, she advises you on how to make your trip to Paris easier.

Now European correspondent for *Gourmet,* **Alexander Lobrano,** who updated the dining and nightlife chapters, has lived in Paris for 14 years. Along with reporting on French food and style for many publications—including *Departures* and *Paris Time Out*—he has also been editor of the *Paris Zagat's Survey.*

Christopher Mooney came to Paris to study French philosophy and hang out in cafés. Nine years later he's still there, but his taste for Gallic thought and tobacco has given way to an unslakable thirst for French wine. A born-again Epicurean, he herein devotes his efforts to finding the best accommodations in Paris.

Ian Phillips, who updated the Outdoor Activities and Sports and Shopping chapters, swiftly made his way around the French capital after moving from England—in his first three years in Paris he lived in 13 different apartments. But he has now found his footing as a freelance journalist, writing on culture and fashion for publications in Paris, London, and New York.

Don't Forget to Write

Keeping a travel guide fresh and up-to-date is a big job. So we love your feedback—positive and negative—and follow up on all suggestions. Contact the Paris editor at editors@fodors.com or c/o Fodor's, 280 Park Avenue, New York, New York 10017. And have a wonderful trip!

Karen Cure

Editorial Director

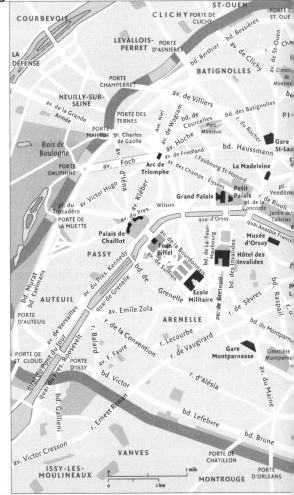

COURBEVOIE

ST-OUEN

CLICHY PORTE DE
CLICHY

PORTE DE
ST-OUE

LEVALLOIS-
PERRET

PORTE
D'ASNIÈRES

bd. Berthier

av. de Clichy

av. de St-Ouen

Cha

LA
DÉFENSE

bd. Bessières

Cimetiè
de
Montmè

PORTE
CHAMPERRET

BATIGNOLLES

NEUILLY-SUR-
SEINE

av. de la Grande
Armée

av. de Villiers

PORTE DES
TERNES

PORTE
MAILLOT

pl. Charles
de Gaulle

Ave. Niel

av. de Wagram

bd. de
Courcelles

Parc
Monceau

bd. des Batignolles

r. du Rocher

PI

Gare
St-La

Bois de
Boulogne

av. Hoche

bd. Haussmann

PORTE
DAUPHINE

av. Foch

Arc de
Triomphe

av. de Friedland

av. des Champs - Élysées

r. Faubourg St-Honoré

La Madeleine

pl.
Vendôm

pl. du
Trocadéro

av. Victor Hugo

av. d'Iéna

av. av. Kléber

Grand Palais

Petit
Palais

pl. de la
Concorde

r. de Rivoli

Jardin de
Tuileries

PORTE DE
LA MUETTE

av. du Pres.

Wilson

Palais de
Chaillot

quai d'Orsay

Musée
d'Orsay

quai Anatole France

PASSY

av. de la Bourdonnais

Tour
Eiffel

av. de Suffren

bd. de La-Tour-
Maubourg

bd. des Invalides

Hôtel des
Invalides

bd. Murat

bd. Exelmans

av. du Pres. Kennedy

bd. de

quai de Grenelle

Grenelle

École
Militaire

av. de Breteuil

r. de Sèvres

bd. Raspail

P
L

AUTEUIL

av. Emile Zola

ARENELLE

PORTE
D'AUTEUIL

av. de Versailles

quai du Pres. Roosevelt

r. Balard

r. de la Convention

r. Lecourbe

r. de Vaugirard

bd. du Montparn

PORTE DE
ST. CLOUD

quai du Pont du Jour

PORTE
D'ISSY

av. F. Faure

Gare
Montparnasse

Cimetière
Montparno

bd. Victor

r. d'Alésia

av. du Maine

bd. Galliéni

r. Ernest Renan

bd. Lefebvre

bd. Brune

av. Victor Cresson

VANVES

PORTE DE
CHATILLON

ISSY-LES-
MOULINEAUX

1 mile

0   1 km

MONTROUGE

PORTE
D'ORLEANS

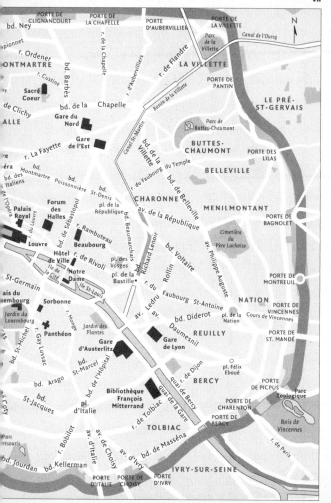

paris with arrondissements

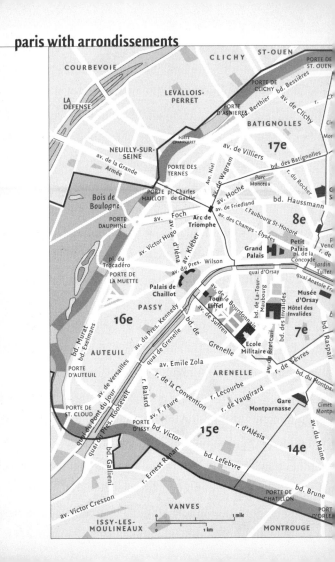

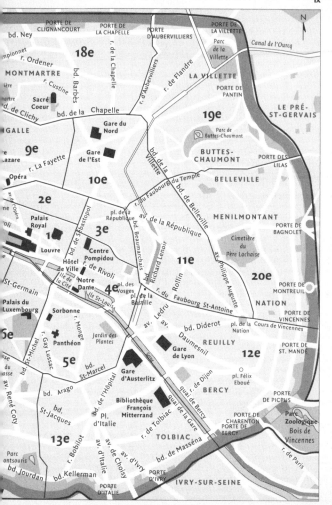

paris métro

Méteor

Gabriel Péri (Asnières-Gennevilliers) 13 14

Mairie de Clichy

Carrefour Pleyel
Mairie de St-Ouen
St-Ouen
St-Denis Porte de Pa

Porte Clignanco

Garibaldi

Seine

Porte de Clichy

Porte de St-Ouen

Guy Môquet

Brochant

Pigalle

La Fourche

Pont de Levallois-Bécon 3

Anatole-France

Place de Clichy

Notre-Dame-de-Lorette

Rome

St-Lazare

Le Peletier
Chaussée-d'Antin
La Fayette

Louise-Michel

Wagram

Malesherbes

Villiers

Europe

Havre-Caumartin

4 S

Porte de Champerret

Péreire

Monceau

Courcelles

St-Augustin

Opéra

Grande Arche de La Défense 1

Esplanade de La Défense

RER LINE A

Charles de Gaulle Étoile

Ternes

St-Philippe-du-Roule

Miromesnil

Madeleine

Concorde

Tuileries

Pont de Neuilly

Les Sablons

Pont Maillot

Argentine

Victor Hugo

George V

F.D. Roosevelt

Champs-Élysées Clemenceau

Musée d'Orsay

Porte Dauphine 2

Kléber

6

Alma-Marceau

Av. Foch

Boissière

Iéna

Invalides

Assemblée Nationale

Solférino

Av. Henri Martin

R. de la Pompe

Trocadéro

Pont de l'Alma

Varenne

Rue du Bac

La Muette

Passy

La Tour-Maubourg

St-François Xavier

Sèvres Babyle

Boulainvilliers

Kennedy Radio France

Bir-Hakeim

Duroc

Vaneau

Ranelagh

Champ-de-Mars Tour Eiffel

Jasmin

Michel-Ange Auteuil

Église d'Auteuil

École Mil.

Ségur

Plac

Porte d'Auteuil

Dupleix

Cambronne

Sèvres Lecourbe

Falguière

Boulogne Jean-Jaurès 10

Michel-Ange-Molitor

Chardon Lagache

Mirabeau

Javel

Charles Michels

La Motte-Picquet-Grenelle

Pasteur

Montparn Bien

Boulogne-Pt. de St-Cloud

Exelmans

Javel André-Citroën

Émile Zola

Avenue Émile

Commerce

Volontaires

Ga

Boucicaut

Félix Faure

Vaugirard

Pe

Boulevard Victor

Lourmel

Convention

Porte de Va

Plais

Balard 8

Porte de Versailles

Malak Plateau de Va

Porte de St-Cloud

Issy Plaine

Corentin Celton

Malak Rue Étienne Do

Marcel Sembat

RER LINE C

Châtillon Montroug

Billancourt

Pont de Sèvres 9

Mairie d'Issy 12

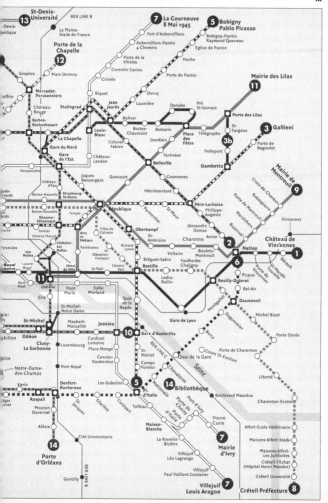

paris

In This Section

introducing paris

IT IS MIDNIGHT at the neighborhood brasserie. Waiters swathed in starchy white glance discreetly at their watches as a family—mother, son, and wife—sip the last of a bottle of Chiroubles and scrape up the remains of their steak tartare on silverware dexterously poised with arched wrists. They are all wearing scarves: The mother's is a classic silk *carré*, tastefully folded at the throat; the wife's is Indian gauze and glitters; the son's is wool and hangs like a prayer shawl over his black turtleneck. Finished, they stir their coffee without looking. They smoke: the mother, Gitanes; the son, Marlboros; the wife rolls her own from a silver case. Alone, they act out their personal theater, uncontrived and unobserved, their Doisneauesque tableau reflected only in the etched-glass mirrors around them, enhanced by the sobriety of their dress and the pallor of their Gallic skin.

Whoever first said that "God found Paris too perfect, so he invented the Parisians," had it wrong. This extraordinary maquette of a city, with its landscape of mansards and chimneys, its low-slung bridges and vast boulevards, is nothing but a rough-sketched stage set that drinks its color from the lifeblood of those infamous Parisians whom everyone claims to hate, but whom everyone loves to emulate.

Mythologized for their arrogance, charm, and savoir faire—as well as their disdain for the foreigners they find genetically incapable of sharing these characteristics—the Parisians continue to mesmerize. For the generations of American and English voyeurs who have ventured curiously, enviously into countless mirrored brasseries, downed numerous bottles of *cuvée maison*, fumbled at nautical knots in newly bought scarves, even suffered squashed berets and unfiltered Gauloises, the Parisian remains imitable—and infinitely fascinating.

Alternately patronizing and self-effacing, they move through their big-city lives with enviable style and urban grit. They are chronically thin, despite the truckloads of beef stew, pâté, and *tarte Tatin* they consume without blushing. They still make the cigarette look glamorous—and a graceful bit of stage business indispensable to good talk—in spite of the gas-mask levels of smoke they generate. They stride over bridges aloof to the mountains framed in every sweeping perspective, yet they discourse—lightly, charmingly—on Racine, NATO, and the latest ruling of the Académie Française. They are proud, practical, often witty and always chic, from the thrift-shop style of the Sorbonne student to the Chanel suit on the thin shoulders of a well-boned *dame d'un certain âge*.

Ferociously (with some justice) in love with their own culture—theater, literature, film, art, architecture, haute cuisine, and haute couture—Parisians worship France as ardently as New Yorkers dismiss the rest of America. While Manhattanites berate the nonentities west of the Hudson, Parisians romanticize the rest of France, making an art of the weekend foray and the regional vacation: Why should we go *à l'étranger* (abroad) when we have the Dordogne, the Auvergne, and Bretagne?

And for all their vulnerability to what they frame as the "American Assault," for every Disney store, action film, and McDonald's in Paris (not to mention Benetton and Laura Ashley, and France's own Celio, Orcade, and Descamps chains), there is a plethora of unique shops selling all-white blouses, African bracelets, dog jackets, and Art Deco jewelry.

And for every commercial bookstore chain there are five tiny *libraries* selling tooled-leather encyclopedias, collections of out-of-print plays, and yellow paperbacks lovingly pressed in waxed paper. The famous *bouquinistes* hover like squatters along the Seine, their folding metal boxes opening to showcase a treasure trove of old magazines, scholarly journals, and hand-colored botanical prints that flap from clothespins in the wind. Yet they are not nomads, these bouquinistes: Dormant through winter, their metal stands are fixtures as permanent and respectable as those of the medieval merchants that built shops along the Pont Neuf. They are determinedly Parisian—individual, independent, and one-of-a-kind.

But in spite of their fierce individuality, Parisians also demand that certain conformities be followed. And here the gap between native and visitor widens. If Parisians treat tourists a bit like occupying forces—disdainfully selling them Beaujolais-Nouveau in July, seating them by the kitchen doors, refusing to understand honest attempts at French—they have formed their opinions based on bitter experience. The waiter who scorches tourists with flared nostrils and firmly turned back was trained to respect his métier—meaning not pouring Coke with foie gras or bringing the check with dessert. The meal is a sacred ritual here and diverging from the norm is tantamount to disgrace.

Doing as the Parisians do, you can go a long way toward closing the gap of disdain. When dining, for example, give yourself over to the meal. Order a kir as an aperitif, instead of a whiskey or beer. Drink wine or mineral water with your meal. Order coffee *after* dessert, not with it. And accept the fact that diet sodas are rarely available in restaurants.

The wine will come chilled, aired, and ready for tasting with the respect usually reserved for a holy relic. Enjoy each course, sipping, discussing, digesting leisurely; the waiter will not be pressed by hurried tourists. When you're done eating, align your silverware on the plate (a sign for the waiter to clear). Cheese can be the climax of the meal, well worth skipping dessert if necessary, and a magnificent way to finish the wine. Have your coffee, without exception, black with sugar; a milky froth will not do on a full stomach. The art of stirring *un express* in Paris rivals the art of scarf-tying.

Ask for *l'addition*; the waiter will not commit the gaffe of bringing the check uninvited. And no matter how deeply you enter into your role as Parisian manqué, avoid saying "Garçon!" (Say "s'il vous plaît" instead.) These are rules that apply at the most unassuming corner bistro and the grandest three-star restaurant; following them can thaw the waiterly chill that can render a meal unforgettable—for all the wrong reasons—and can make for meals that are memorable as an evening at the Opéra de la Bastille, complete with sets and choreography.

It is this fixed attention to experience and detail that sets the Parisians apart. Desk-eaters they are not: When they work, they work without a coffee break. When they eat, business still grinds to a halt. Weekends are sacred. And oh, do they vacation, all of them at once, all of them abandoning Paris in August with a fierceness of purpose that mirrors their commitment to food— an all-night drive, a rental booked months in advance.

By matching that Parisian passion for the complete, the correct, the comme il faut, your own experience will be all the more authentic. Having eaten with proper reverence, keep your sightseeing agenda at the same lofty level. If you go to the Louvre, spend the day; do not lope through the wide corridors in search of *La Joconde* (Mona Lisa). You can leave for a three-hour lunch, if you choose, and come back with the same ticket, even avoiding the lines by reentering via the Passage Richelieu. If time won't allow an all-day survey, do as the locals do: Choose an era and immerse yourself. Then take a break and plunge into another. Eavesdrop on a guided tour. Go back and look at a painting again. And take the time to stare at the ceilings: The architecture alone of this historic monument merits a day's tour.

As you apply yourself to the Parisian experience in spirit, diverge in fact: Walk. The natives may prefer to sit in a café or even hurry straight home by métro ("*métro, boulot, dodo*"—"métro, work, sleep"—as the saying goes). You, as a visitor, are obliged to wander down tortuous medieval streets; up vast boulevards so overscaled you seem to gain no ground; over bridges that open up to broad perspectives on illuminated monuments that outnumber even those in Rome.

They are all there, the clichés of Paris romance: The moon over the Seine reflected in the wake of the Bateaux Mouches; the steps Leslie Caron blushed down in *An American in Paris*; the lovers kissing under the lime tree pollards. But there are surprises, too: a troop of hunting horns striking unearthly sonorities under a resonant bridge; flocks of wild geese flying low over the towers of Notre-Dame; and a ragged expatriate-writer leaving a well-scraped plat du jour on the table as he bolts away from the bill.

The more resourceful you are, the more surprises you will unearth in your Paris wanderings. Follow the strains of Lully into a chamber orchestra rehearsal in St-Julien-le-Pauvre; if you're quiet and still, you may not be asked to leave. Brave the smoking lounge at intermission at the Comédie Française and you'll find the battered leather chair that the young actor Molière sat in as *L'Invalide Imaginaire*. Take the métro to *L'Armée du Salut* (Salvation Army) in the 13ᵉ arrondissement, and you'll not only find Art Deco percolators and hand-knit stockings, but you'll also be inside the futuristic curves of a 1933 Le Corbusier masterwork.

Tear yourself away from the big-name museums and you'll discover a world of small galleries. Go in: You don't have to press your nose to the glass. The exhibits are constantly changing and you can always find one relevant to Paris—Frank Horvat's photos of Pigalle or a Christo retrospective, including the Pont Neuf wrappings. It is worth buying one of the weekly guides— *Pariscope, Les Officiels des Spectacles, Figaroscope*—and browsing through it over your *café crème* and croissant.

Resourcefulness, after all, is a sign of enthusiasm and appreciation—for when you are well informed and acutely tuned in to the nuances of the city, you can approach it as a connoisseur. Then you can peacefully coexist with Parisians, partaking in their passion for this marvelous old city, from the same plate of cultural riches. Hemingway, as usual, put it succinctly: "It was always pleasant crossing bridges in Paris." Cultural bridges, too. Bon séjour à Paris.

—Nancy Coons

A frequent contributor to Fodor's, Nancy Coons has written on food and culture for National Geographic Traveler, Wall Street Journal, Opera News, and European Travel & Life. Based in Luxembourg and France since 1987, she now works out of her 300-year-old farmhouse in Lorraine, which she shares with her husband and two daughters.

PLEASURES AND PASTIMES

CAFÉS

Some would say people-watching is what Paris is all about; and there's no better place to indulge in this pursuit than at a sidewalk café. Favored locales include place St-Michel, boulevard du Montparnasse, and place St-Germain-des-Prés, on the Left Bank; and place de l'Opéra, the Champs-Élysées, and Les Halles, on the Right Bank. But you may enjoy seeking out your own (less expensive) local haunts.

CHURCHES

Paris is rich in churches of two architectural styles: the 15th- to 16th-century overlap of Flamboyant Gothic and Renaissance (at St-Gervais, St-Étienne du Mont, St-Eustache, and St-Séverin) and 17th-century Baroque with domes and two-tiered facades (at Les Invalides, Val de Grâce, and St-Paul–St-Louis). But the city's most enduring religious symbols are medieval (Sainte-

Chapelle and the cathedral of Notre-Dame) and 19th-century (Sacré-Coeur and La Madeleine).

DINING

As for dining, well. . . the French wrote the book. Paris is one of the world's great food capitals and a bastion of classic French cuisine. Nonetheless, if you're coming from New York, London, or Los Angeles, where innovative restaurants abound, you may find the French capital a little staid. In fact, a battle is currently being waged between the traditionalists and a remarkable new generation of chefs who are modernizing French cooking—and changing the French culinary landscape. In the end, fads and trends may come and go, but the pragmatic Parisian will always know that this city sets the standards.

MUSEUMS

You'll find Leonardos, Monets, and Toulouse-Lautrecs tossed into one bright bouquet when you go museum-hopping in Paris. Alongside the superstars—the Louvre, the Musée d'Orsay, and the newly renovated Centre Pompidou—are such delights as the Musée National du Moyen Age (displaying medieval works of art in the famous Hôtel de Cluny), the regal Louis Quinze splendor of the Musée Nissim de Camondo, and single-artist museums dedicated to the works of Picasso, Rodin, Dalí, and Maillol.

SHOPPING

Whether you decide to bargain at a flea-market or go whole-snob on the Place Vendôme, shopping opportunities in Paris are endless and geared to every taste. You can spend an afternoon browsing through bookstalls along the Seine, shopping for one of Hermès's famous *foulards* (scarves), touring high-gloss department stores, or bargaining over prices in the sprawling flea markets on the outskirts of town. Everywhere you turn, tastefully displayed wares—luscious chocolates, exquisite clothing, gleaming copper pots—entice the eye and fire the imagination.

QUICK TOURS

If you're here for just a short stay, you need to plan carefully so as to make the most of your time in Paris. The following itineraries outline major sights throughout the city, and will help you structure your visit efficiently. Each is intended to take about four hours—perfect to fill a free morning or afternoon. For more information about individual sights, *see* Here and There.

ARC DE TRIOMPHE TO THE LOUVRE

Start at the **Arc de Triomphe;** from the top there's a great view of the city and the boulevards emanating from the Étoile. With the arch as your starting point, the rest of your walk will be all downhill. Work your way along the **Champs-Élysées,** across **place de la Concorde** and the **Tuileries Garden** (with the notable **Jeu de Paume** museum if you have an hour to spare) to the **Louvre.** Note that a tour of the Louvre's galleries could easily take half a day on its own.

EIFFEL TOWER AND THE MUSÉE D'ORSAY

West of the École Militaire métro stop, the verdant expanse of the **Champ de Mars** provides a thrilling approach to the **Tour Eiffel.** After you ascend the famous tower (early morning is best to avoid crowds), you can easily spend the rest of a morning or afternoon admiring the vast holdings of the **Musée d'Orsay.** To get to the museum from the Eiffel Tower, walk east along the Seine to the Pont de l'Alma station and take the RER two stops to the Musée d'Orsay.

THE GRAND BOULEVARDS

For *très chic* shopping and a look at Haussmann's 19th-century Paris, walk down the Right Bank's **Faubourg St-Honoré** from the Miromesnil or Concorde métro stations. Turn left (north) on rue Royale and join the Grand Boulevards by the **Madeleine** church; continue northeast along the boulevards past the **Opéra Garnier** toward **place de la République.**

THE LEFT BANK

From the Cluny-La Sorbonne métro stop, explore the **Latin Quarter.** You can stroll around the academic center of Paris, near the **Sorbonne,** and then walk along boulevard St-Michel. If you walk south, the boulevard will take you to the **Panthéon** (via rue Soufflot) and the **Jardin du Luxembourg.** To the north, boulevard St-Michel crosses a main artery—boulevard St-Germain—before it ends at place St-Michel and the Seine. For a look at some worthwhile shops and galleries and an open-air food marked (on rue de Buci), walk west along boulevard St-Germain toward the Odéon métro stop, then turn north or south onto one of several enticing narrow and winding roads.

MONTMARTRE

Take the métro to Anvers and head up bustling rue de Steinkerque; the **Sacré-Coeur Basilica** looms overhead. Take the funicular to the top. Walk west through **place du Tertre** and along rue Lepic. Then head south along rue Tholozé to rue des Abbesses and **place des Abbesses,** where you'll find two gems of Art Nouveau: the church St-Jean de Montmartre, and the famous Guimard entrance to the Abbesses métro station.

NOTRE-DAME, THE ISLANDS, AND THE MARAIS

Begin your tour on **Ile de la Cité** with a visit to **Notre-Dame Cathedral** and, if you enjoy medieval architecture, the **Ste-Chapelle** to the west. Head back toward Notre-Dame, then cross the Seine at Pont Louis and wander around villagelike **Ile St-Louis,** using rue de St-Louis-en-l'Ile as your main axis. If you've still got some time left, backtrack west to Pont Louis-Philippe and walk north to the Marais via rue du Pont Louis-Philippe and rue Vieille du Temple.

In This Section

Revised and updated by Simon Hewitt

here and there

A CITY OF VAST, noble perspectives and winding, hidden streets, Paris remains a combination of the pompous and the intimate. Whether you've come looking for sheer physical beauty, cultural and artistic diversions, world-famous dining and shopping, history, or simply local color, you will find it here in abundance.

As world capitals go, Paris is surprisingly compact. With the exceptions of the Bois de Boulogne and Montmartre, you can easily walk from one major sight to the next. The city is divided in two by the River Seine, with two islands (the Ile de la Cité and Ile St-Louis) in the middle. Each bank of the Seine has its own personality; the Rive Droite (Right Bank), with its spacious boulevards and formal buildings, generally has a more genteel feel than the carefree Rive Gauche (Left Bank), to the south. The east–west axis from Châtelet to the Arc de Triomphe, via the rue de Rivoli and the Champs-Élysées, is the Right Bank's principal thoroughfare for sightseeing and shopping.

The city is divided into 20 *arrondissements* (districts). The last two digits of a city zip code (e.g., 75002) will tell you the arrondissement (in this case, the 2e, or 2nd). Although the best method of getting to know Paris is on foot, public transportation—particularly the métro system—is excellent. Buy the *Plan de Paris* booklet, a city map and guide with a street-name index that also shows métro stations. Note that all métro stations have a detailed neighborhood map just inside the entrance.

Our coverage of Paris is divided into nine neighborhoods. There are several must-sees that you don't want to miss: the Eiffel Tower, the Arc de Triomphe, the Louvre, and Notre-Dame. A few monuments and museums close for lunch, between noon and 2, and many are closed on either Monday or Tuesday: Check before you set off. Admission prices listed are for adults, but often there are special rates for students, children, and senior citizens.

FROM NOTRE-DAME TO THE PLACE DE LA CONCORDE

No matter how you first approach Paris—historically, geographically, emotionally—it is the River Seine that summons us and that harbors two celebrated islands, the Ile de la Cité and the Ile St-Louis, both at the very center of the city. Of the two, it is the Ile de la Cité that forms the historic ground zero of Paris. It was here that the earliest inhabitants of Paris, the Gaulish tribe of the Parisii, settled in about 250 BC, calling their home Lutetia, meaning "settlement surrounded by water." Today it is famed for the great, brooding cathedral of Notre-Dame, the haunted Conciergerie, and the dazzling Sainte-Chapelle. If Notre-Dame represents Church, another major attraction of this walk—the Louvre—symbolizes State. A succession of French rulers was responsible for filling this immense, symmetrical structure with the world's greatest paintings and works of art, now the largest museum in the world, as well as one of the easiest to get lost in. Beyond the Louvre lie the lovely Tuileries Gardens, the grand place de la Concorde—the very hub of the city—and the Belle Epoque splendor of the Grand Palais and the Pont Alexandre III. All in all, this area comprises some of the most historic and beautiful sights to see in Paris.

Numbers in the margin correspond to the numbers on the Notre-Dame to the Place de la Concorde map; these numbers indicate a suggested path for sightseeing.

Sights to See

8 CARROUSEL DU LOUVRE. Part of the early '90s Louvre renovation program, this subterranean shopping complex is centered on an inverted glass pyramid (overlooked by the regional Ile-de-France tourist office) and contains a wide range of stores, spaces for fashion shows, an auditorium, and a huge parking garage. At lunchtime, museum visitors rush to the mall-style food court, where fast food goes international. Note that you can get into or exit from the museum (and avoid some lines) by entering through the mall. *Entrances on rue de Rivoli or by Arc du Carrousel. Métro: Palais-Royal.*

4 CONCIERGERIE. This turreted medieval building by the Seine was originally part of the royal palace on Ile de la Cité. Most people know it, however, as the prison whence Danton, Robespierre, and Marie-Antoinette were bundled off to the guillotine. You can visit Marie-Antoinette's cell, the guardroom, and the monumental Salle des Gens d'Armes (Hall of Men-at-Arms). *1 quai de l'Horloge, tel. 01–53–73–78–50. 25 frs; joint ticket with Sainte-Chapelle 50 frs. Spring–fall, daily 9:30–6:30; winter, daily 10–5. Métro: Cité.*

12 GRAND PALAIS (Grand Palace). With its curved glass roof, the Grand Palais is unmistakable when approached from either the Seine or the Champs-Élysées and forms an attractive duo with the **Petit Palais,** on the other side of avenue Winston-Churchill. Although undergoing renovation until 2002, it also houses the Palais de la Découverte (☞ *below*)—home to the city planetarium—which can be visited. *Av. Winston-Churchill, tel. 01–42–65–12–73. 27 frs. Tues.–Sun. 10–5:40. Métro: Champs-Élysées-Clemenceau.*

9 JARDIN DES TUILERIES (Tuileries Gardens). Immortalized in Impressionist canvases by Monet and Pissarro, the Tuileries Gardens are typically French: formal and neatly patterned, with rows of trees, gravel paths, flower beds, and a host of statues from

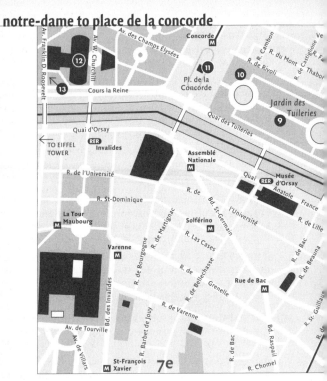

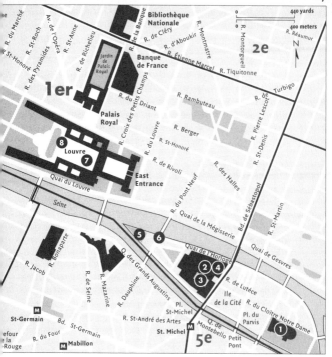

0   440 yards
0   400 meters

2e

N

R. du Marché
R. St-Roch
Av. de l'Opéra
R. St-Anne
R. des Pyramides
St-Honoré
R. de Richelieu
de la Banque

Bibliothèque Nationale

R. de Cléry
R. d'Aboukir
R. Montmartre
R. Étienne Marcel
R. Tiquitonne
R. Montorgueil
R. Réaumur

Jardin de Palais Royal

Banque de France

1er

R. du Louvre
R. Croix des Petits Champs
R. Rambuteau
R. Pierre Lescot
R. de Turbigo

Palais Royal

R. Berger
R. St-Honoré
R. de Rivoli
R. St-Denis
R. des Halles
Bd. de Sébastopol

8
Louvre
7

East Entrance

R. St-Martin

Quai du Louvre

Seine

R. du Pont Neuf

Quai de la Mégisserie

Quai de Gesvres

5 **6**

R. Bonaparte
R. Jacob
R. de Seine
R. Mazarine
Q. des Grands Augustins
R. Dauphine

Quai de l'Horloge

2 **4**
3

R. de Lutèce

Ile de la Cité

R. du Cloître Notre Dame

Pl. St-Michel

Pl. du Parvis

1

Ⓜ **St-Germain**
Bd. St-Germain
R. St-André des Artes

St. Michel Ⓜ

Q. de Montebello

efour
e la
-Rouge
R. du Four
Ⓜ **Mabillon**

5e

Petit Pont

varying eras. This is a delightful place to stroll and survey the surrounding cityscape. *Métro: Concorde, Tuileries.*

❼ LOUVRE. Leonardo da Vinci's *Mona Lisa* and *Virgin and St. Anne*, Veronese's *Marriage at Cana*, Giorgione's *Concert Champêtre*, Delacroix's *Liberty Guiding the People*, Whistler's *Mother (Arrangement in Black and White)*. . . you get the picture. This is the world's greatest art museum and certainly one of the largest. Today, after three decades of renovations, the Louvre is now a coherent, unified structure, and search parties no longer need to be sent in to bring you out. Originally built by Philippe-Auguste in the 13th century as a fortress, it was not until the reign of pleasure-loving François I, 300 years later, that today's Louvre gradually began to take shape. Through the years Henri IV (1589–1610), Louis XIII (1610–43), Louis XIV (1643–1715), Napoléon (1804–14), and Napoléon III (1852–70) all contributed to its construction. The recent history of the Louvre centers on I. M. Pei's glass pyramid, unveiled in March 1989, and numerous renovations.

The number one attraction is Leonardo da Vinci's enigmatic **Mona Lisa** (*La Joconde*, to the French); be forewarned that you will find it encased in glass and surrounded by a mob of tourists. (You might be better off forsaking her rather dour image and plunking yourself in front of Leonardo's *Virgin and St. Anne*, which contains two of the most beautiful faces the artist ever painted.) The collections are divided into seven sections: Asian antiquities; Egyptian antiquities; Greek and Roman antiquities; sculpture; paintings, prints, and drawings; furniture; and objets d'art. Don't try to see it all at once; try, instead, to make repeat visits—the admission is nearly half price on Sunday and after 3 PM on other days. (Unless you plan on going to a number of museums every day, the one-, three-, and five-day tourist museum passes probably aren't worth your money since you could easily spend a whole day at the Louvre alone.) Some other highlights of the paintings are *Shepherds in Arcadia*, by Nicolas Poussin (1594–1665); *The Oath of the Horatii*, by Jacques-Louis

David (1748–1825); and *La Grande Odalisque,* by Jean-Auguste-Dominique Ingres (1780–1867). The French crown jewels (in the objets d'art section of the Richelieu Wing) include the mind-boggling 186-carat Regent diamond. The Nike, or *Winged Victory of Samothrace,* seems poised for flight at the top of the stairs, and another much-loved piece of sculpture is Michelangelo's pair of *Slaves,* intended for the tomb of Pope Julius II. These can be admired in the Denon Wing, where a new medieval and Renaissance sculpture section is housed partly in the former imperial stables. In 1997 new rooms for Persian, Arab, Greek, and Egyptian art were opened. Come as early as possible to avoid the crowds. *Palais du Louvre (other than the main entrance at the Pei pyramid, you can also enter through the East Front and through the Carrousel du Louvre mall on rue de Rivoli), tel. 01–40–20–51–51. 45 frs; 26 frs after 3 pm and on Sun.; free 1st Sun. of month. Thurs.–Sun. 9–6, Mon. and Wed. 9 am–9:45 pm. Some sections open limited days. Métro: Palais-Royal.*

⑩ MUSÉE DU JEU DE PAUME. At the entrance to the Tuileries Garden, this museum is an ultramodern white-walled showcase for excellent temporary exhibits of bold contemporary art. Its adjoining sister museum, the **Musée de l'Orangerie**—home to Claude Monet's largest *Water Lilies*—is closed for renovation until 2002. *1 pl. de la Concorde, tel. 01–42–60–69–69. 38 frs. Tues. noon–9:30, Wed.–Fri. noon–7, weekends 10–7. Métro: Concorde.*

★ ❶ NOTRE-DAME. Looming above the large, pedestrian place du Parvis is Notre-Dame Cathedral, the most enduring symbol of Paris. Begun in 1163, it was not completed until 1345. The facade seems perfectly proportioned until you notice that the north (left) tower is wider than the south tower. The south tower houses the great bell of Notre-Dame, as tolled by Quasimodo, Victor Hugo's fictional hunchback. The cathedral interior, with its vast proportions, soaring nave, and soft multicolor light filtering through the stained-glass windows, inspires awe despite the inevitable throngs of tourists. Visit early in the morning, when the cathedral is at its lightest and least crowded. Window space is limited and filled with shimmering stained glass; the circular rose windows in the transept are particularly delicate. The 387-step climb up the towers is worth the effort for a perfect view of the famous gargoyles and the heart of Paris. *Pl. du Parvis. Towers 35 frs. Cathedral 8 am–7 pm; towers summer, daily 9:30–7:30; winter, daily 10–5. Métro: Cité.*

👆 ⑬ **PALAIS DE LA DÉCOUVERTE** (Palace of Discovery). A planetarium, working models, and scientific and technological exhibits on such topics as optics, biology, nuclear physics, and electricity make up this science museum behind the Grand Palais. *Av. Franklin-D.-Roosevelt, tel. 01–56–43–20–21. 30 frs, 15 frs extra for planetarium. Tues.–Sat. 9:30–6, Sun. 10–7. Métro: Champs-Élysées–Clemenceau.*

② **PALAIS DE JUSTICE** (Law Courts). In about 1860 the city law courts were built by Baron Haussmann in his characteristically weighty Neoclassical style. You can wander around the buildings, watch the bustle of the lawyers, or attend a court hearing. But the real interest here is the medieval part of the complex, spared by Haussmann: La Conciergerie and Ste-Chapelle (☞ *above and below*, respectively). *Bd. du Palais. Métro: Cité.*

⑪ **PLACE DE LA CONCORDE.** This majestic square at the foot of the Champs-Élysées was laid out in the 1770s, but there was nothing in the way of peace or concord about its early years. Between 1793 and 1795 more than a thousand victims, including Louis XVI and Marie-Antoinette, were slashed into oblivion at the guillotine, prompting Madame Roland to famously cry, "Liberty, what crimes are committed in thy name." The top of the 107-ft **Obelisk**—a present from the viceroy of Egypt in 1833—was regilded in 1998. *Métro: Concorde.*

⑥ **PONT NEUF** (New Bridge). Crossing the Ile de la Cité, just behind square du Vert-Galant, is the oldest bridge in Paris, confusingly called the New Bridge, or Pont Neuf. It was completed in 1607 and was the first bridge in the city to be built without houses lining either side. *Métro: Pont-Neuf.*

★ ❸ **SAINTE-CHAPELLE** (Holy Chapel). One of the most magical sights in European medieval art, this chapel was built by Louis IX (1226–70; later canonized as St. Louis) in the 1240s to house what he believed to be Christ's Crown of Thorns, purchased from Emperor Baldwin of Constantinople. A dark and gloomy lower chapel is the prelude to the shimmering upper one, whose walls consist of little but dazzling 13th-century stained glass. Think of it as an enormous magic lantern, illuminating 1,130 figures from the Bible, to create—as one writer put it—"the most marvelous colored and moving air ever held within four walls." 4 bd. du Palais, tel. 01–43–54–30–09 for concert information. 35 frs; joint ticket with Conciergerie 50 frs. Apr.–Sept., daily 9:30–6:30; Oct.–Mar., daily 10–5. *Métro: Cité.*

❺ **SQUARE DU VERT-GALANT.** The equestrian statue of the Vert-Galant himself—amorous adventurer Henri IV—surveys this leafy square at the western end of the Ile de la Cité. Henri, king of France from 1589 until his assassination in 1610, is probably best remembered for his cynical remark that *"Paris vaut bien une messe"* ("Paris is worth a mass"), a reference to his readiness to renounce Protestantism to gain the throne of predominantly Catholic France. A fine spot to linger on a sunny afternoon, the square is also the departure point for the glass-top vedettes (tour boats) on the Seine (at the bottom of the steps to the right). *Métro: Pont-Neuf.*

FROM THE EIFFEL TOWER TO THE ARC DE TRIOMPHE

The Eiffel Tower lords over southwest Paris, and wherever you are on this walk, you can see it looming overhead. Water is the second theme: fountains playing beneath place du Trocadéro and tours along the Seine on a Bateau Mouche. Museums are the third: The area around Trocadéro is full of them. And style is the fourth, but not just because the buildings here are

eiffel tower to the arc de triomphe

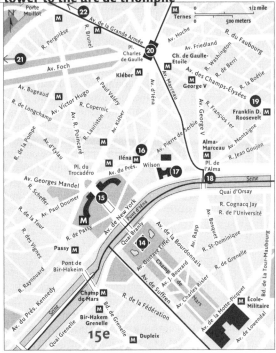

overwhelmingly elegant—this is also the center of haute couture, with the top names in world fashion all congregated around avenue Montaigne, only a brief walk from the Champs-Élysées, to the north.

Numbers in the margin correspond to the numbers on the Eiffel Tower to the Arc de Triomphe map; these numbers indicate a suggested path for sightseeing.

Sights to See

★ ⑳ **ARC DE TRIOMPHE.** This huge arch, standing 164 ft, was planned by Napoléon but not finished until 1836, 20 years after the end of his rule. It is decorated with some magnificent sculptures by François Rude, such as the *Departure of the Volunteers*, better known as *La Marseillaise*, to the right of the arch when viewed from the Champs-Élysées. A small museum halfway up the arch is devoted to its history. France's Unknown Soldier is buried beneath the archway; the flame is rekindled every evening at 6:30. *Pl. Charles-de-Gaulle, tel. 01–55–37–73–77. 40 frs. Spring–autumn, daily 9:30 am–11 pm; winter, daily 10 am–10:30 pm. Métro, RER: Charles-de-Gaulle–Étoile.*

⑱ **BATEAUX MOUCHES.** These popular motorboats set off on their hour-long tours of Paris waters regularly (every half hour in summer). *Pl. de l'Alma, tel. 01–40–76–99–99. 40 frs. Métro: Alma-Marceau.*

㉑ **BOIS DE BOULOGNE.** Class and style have been associated with this 2,200-acre wood—known to Parisians as Le Bois—ever since it was landscaped into an upper-class playground by Baron Haussmann in the 1850s. Today, the park is home to rowers, joggers, strollers, riders, picnickers, the racetracks of **Longchamp** and **Auteuil,** the **Roland Garros** stadium (where the French Open tennis tournament is held in late May), and—after dark—ladies of the night. *Main entrance at bottom of av. Foch. Métro: Porte Maillot, Porte Dauphine, Porte d'Auteuil; Bus 244.*

⑲ CHAMPS-ÉLYSÉES. The 2-km (1-mi) Champs-Élysées was originally laid out in the 1660s by landscape gardener André Le Nôtre as parkland sweeping away from the Tuileries. In an attempt to reestablish this thoroughfare as one of the world's most beautiful avenues, the city planted extra trees, broadened sidewalks, refurbished Art Nouveau newsstands, and clamped down on garish storefronts. *Métro: George-V, Champs-Élysées–Clemenceau, Franklin-D.-Roosevelt.*

㉒ LA DÉFENSE. This is the skyscraper district of Paris, located just west of Paris (thankfully) across the Seine from Neuilly. Sights here include a spherical IMAX cinema, the **Musée de l'Automobile** for car fans, and, crowning the main plaza, the **Grande Arche de La Défense,** an enormous open cube of a building, where tubular glass elevators whisk you 360 ft to the top. *Parvis de La Défense, tel. 01–49–07–27–57. Arch 43 frs; auto museum 35 frs. Arch daily 10–7, auto museum daily 12:35–7:30. Métro, RER: Grande Arche de La Défense.*

⑰ MUSÉE D'ART MODERNE DE LA VILLE DE PARIS (City Museum of Modern Art). Both temporary exhibits and a permanent collection of top-quality 20th-century art can be found at this museum. It takes over, chronologically speaking, where the Musée d'Orsay (☞ *below*) leaves off: Among the earliest works are Fauve paintings by Vlaminck and Derain, followed by Picasso's early experiments in Cubism. *11 av. du Président-Wilson, tel. 01–53–67–40–00. 27 frs. Tues.–Fri. 10–5:30, weekends 10–6:45. Métro: Iéna.*

⑯ MUSÉE GUIMET. This Belle Epoque museum was founded by Lyonnais industrialist Émile Guimet, who traveled around the world in the late 19th century amassing Indo-Chinese and Far Eastern objets d'art, plus a fabled collection of Cambodian art. After a massive renovation, the museum reopened in fall 2000. *6 pl. d'Iéna, tel. 01–45–05–00–98. Wed.–Mon. 9:45–6. Métro: Iéna.*

⑮ PALAIS DE CHAILLOT (Chaillot Palace). This honey-color, Art Deco culture center facing the Seine, perched atop tumbling gardens with sculpture and fountains, was built in the 1930s and houses three museums: the **Musée de l'Homme** (Museum of Mankind) with an array of prehistoric artifacts; the **Musée de la Marine** (Maritime Museum), with its salty collection of model ships, marine paintings, and naval paraphernalia; and the **Musée des Monuments Français** (Museum of French Monuments), closed for renovation until 2003. *Pl. du Trocadéro, tel. 01–44–05–72–72 Museum of Mankind; 01–53–65–69–69 Maritime Museum. Museum of Mankind 30 frs; Maritime Museum 38 frs. Museum of Mankind Wed.–Mon. 9:45–5:15; Maritime Museum Wed.–Mon. 10–6. Métro: Trocadéro.*

★ **⑭ TOUR EIFFEL** (Eiffel Tower). Known to the French as La Tour Eiffel (pronounced ef-*el*), Paris's most famous landmark was built by Gustave Eiffel for the World Exhibition of 1889, the centennial of the French Revolution, and was still in good shape to celebrate its own 100th birthday. Such was Eiffel's engineering wizardry that even in the strongest winds his tower never sways more than 4½ inches. If you're full of energy, stride up the stairs as far as the third deck. If you want to go to the top, you'll have to take the elevator. To honor the new millennium, the Tower was transformed into a giant sparkler one second after midnight on January 1st, 2000. The good news is that it will continue to light up every night until January 1st, 2001—every hour on the hour, for ten glittering minutes, from dusk until one AM. *Quai Branly, tel. 01–44–11–23–23. By elevator: 2nd floor, 21 frs; 3rd floor, 43 frs; 4th floor, 60 frs. By foot: 2nd and 3rd floors only, 15 frs. July–Aug., daily 9 am–midnight; Sept.–June, daily 9 am–11 pm. Métro: Bir-Hakeim; RER: Champ-de-Mars.*

THE FAUBOURG ST-HONORÉ

The Faubourg St-Honoré, north of the Champs-Élysées and the Tuileries, is synonymous with style—as you will see as you progress from the President's Palace, past a wealth of art galleries, to the monumental Madeleine church and on to stately place Vendôme, home to the Ritz and the world's top jewelers. Leading names in modern fashion are found farther east on place des Victoires, close to what was for centuries the gastronomic heart of Paris: Les Halles (pronounced lay-*al*), once the city's main market. In 1969 Les Halles was closed and replaced by a park and a modern shopping mall, the Forum des Halles. The brash modernity of the Forum stands in contrast to the august church of St-Eustache nearby. Similarly, the incongruous black-and-white columns, an in-situ artwork created by a Minimalist artist in the 1980s, in the classical courtyard of Richelieu's neighboring Palais-Royal present a further case of daring modernity—or architectural vandalism, depending on your point of view.

Numbers in the margin correspond to the numbers on the Faubourg St-Honoré map; these numbers indicate a suggested path for sightseeing.

Sights to See

30 BOURSE DU COMMERCE (Commercial Exchange). The 18th-century circular, shallow-dome Commercial Exchange, near Les Halles, began life as a corn exchange; Victor Hugo waggishly likened it to a jockey's cap without the peak. *Rue de Viarmes. Métro or RER: Les Halles.*

27 COMÉDIE FRANÇAISE. This theater is the setting for performances of classical French drama. The building itself dates from 1790, but the Comédie Française company was created by that most theatrical of French monarchs, Louis XIV, back in 1680. *Pl. Colette, tel. 01–44–58–15–15. Métro: Palais-Royal.*

24 ÉGLISE DE LA MADELEINE (Church of La Madeleine). With its rows of uncompromising columns, this sturdy neoclassical edifice—designed in 1814 but not consecrated until 1842—looks more like a Greek temple than a Christian church. In fact, La Madeleine, as it is known, was nearly selected as Paris's first train station (the site of the Gare St-Lazare, just up the road, was chosen instead). Inside, the walls are richly and harmoniously decorated; gold glints through the murk. The portico's majestic Corinthian colonnade supports a gigantic pediment with a frieze of the Last Judgment. *Pl. de la Madeleine. Mon.–Sat. 7:30–7, Sun. 8–7. Métro: Madeleine.*

32 **FORUM DES HALLES.** Les Halles, the iron-and-glass halls that made up the central Paris food market, were closed in 1969 and replaced in the late '70s by the Forum des Halles, a mundane shopping mall. Unfortunately, much of its plastic, concrete, glass, and mock-marble exterior is already showing signs of wear and tear. *Main entrance on rue Pierre-Lescot. Métro: Les Halles; RER: Châtelet–Les Halles.*

NEED A BREAK? Founded in 1903, **Angélina** (226 rue de Rivoli, tel. 01–42–60–82–00) is an elegant *salon de thé* (tearoom), famous for its *chocolat africain*, a jug of hot chocolate served with whipped cream (irresistible even in summer).

23 **PALAIS DE L'ÉLYSÉE** (Élysée Palace). This "palace," known to the French simply as L'Élysée, where the French president lives, works, and receives official visitors, was originally constructed as a private mansion in 1718 and has housed presidents only since 1873. Although you can catch a glimpse of the palace forecourt and facade through the Faubourg St-Honoré gateway, it is difficult to get much idea of the building's size or of the extensive gardens that stretch back to the Champs-Élysées. *55 rue du Faubourg–St-Honoré. Not open to public. Métro: Miromesnil.*

28 **PALAIS-ROYAL** (Royal Palace). The buildings of this former palace—royal only in that all-powerful Cardinal Richelieu (1585–1642) magnanimously bequeathed them to Louis XIII—date from the 1630s. Today the Palais-Royal is home to the French Ministry of Culture and private apartments (Colette and Cocteau were two

the faubourg st-honoré

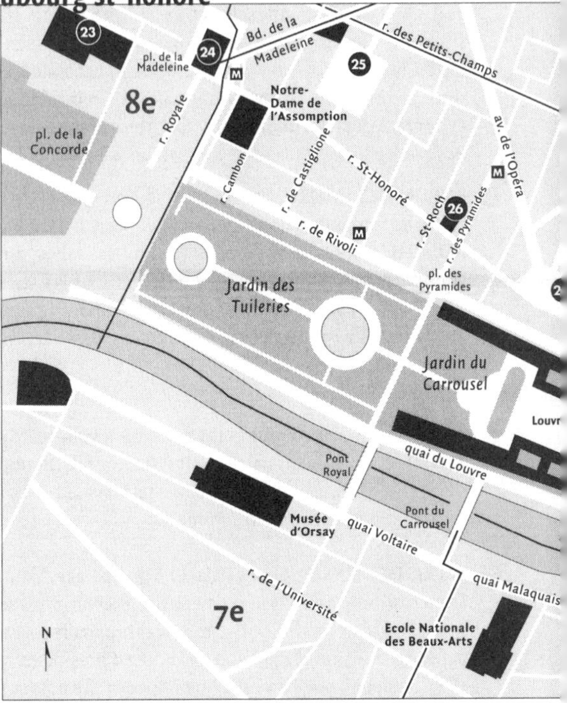

Bd. de la Madeleine

r. des Petits-Champs

(23)

pl. de la Madeleine

(24) M

(25)

8e

r. Royale

Notre-Dame de l'Assomption

av. de l'Opéra

pl. de la Concorde

r. Cambon

r. de Castiglione

r. St-Honoré

r. de Rivoli M

r. St-Roch

(26)

r. des Pyramides

M

pl. des Pyramides

Jardin des Tuileries

2

Jardin du Carrousel

Louvr

quai du Louvre

Pont Royal

Pont du Carrousel

Musée d'Orsay

quai Voltaire

quai Malaquais

r. de l'Université

7e

Ecole Nationale des Beaux-Arts

N

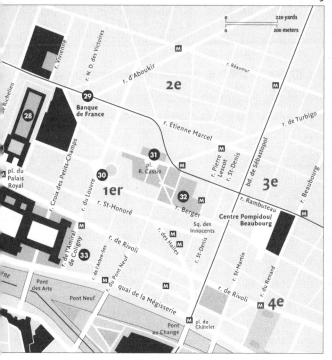

0 | 220 yards
0 | 200 meters

r. Vivienne

r. N. D. des Victoires

r. d'Aboukir

r. Réaumur

2e

de Richelieu

29
Banque
de France

r. de Turbigo

28

r. Etienne Marcel

31
pl.
R. Cassin

r. Pierre
Lescot

r. St-Denis

bd. de Sébastopol

3e

r. de Beaubourg

pl. du
Palais
Royal

r. Croix des Petits-Champs

30

r. du Louvre

1er

r. St-Honoré

32

r. Berger

r. Rambuteau

**Centre Pompidou/
Beaubourg**

Sq. des
Innocents

r. de l'Amiral
de Coligny

33

r. de l'Arbre-Sec

r. de Rivoli

r. des Halles

r. St-Denis

r. St-Martin

r. de Rivoli

r. du Renard

4e

ine

Pont
des Arts

r. du Pont Neuf

Pont Neuf

quai de la Mégisserie

Pont
au Change

pl. du
Châtelet

lucky former owners), and its buildings are not open to the public. You can, however, visit its colonnaded courtyard and classical gardens, a tranquil oasis prized by Parisians. *Pl. du Palais-Royal. Métro: Palais-Royal.*

㉕ PLACE VENDÔME. Mansart's rhythmic, perfectly proportioned example of 17th-century urban architecture shines in all its golden-stone splendor. The square is a fitting showcase for the deluxe Ritz Hotel and the cluster of jewelry display windows found here. Napoléon had the square's central column made from the melted bronze of 1,200 cannons captured at the Battle of Austerlitz in 1805. There he is, perched vigilantly at the top. *Métro: Opéra.*

㉙ PLACE DES VICTOIRES. This circular square, now home to many of the city's top fashion boutiques, was laid out in 1685 by Jules-Hardouin Mansart in honor of the military victories (*victoires*) of Louis XIV. The Sun King gallops along on a bronze horse in the middle. *Métro: Sentier.*

㉛ ST-EUSTACHE. A huge church, it was built as the people's Right Bank reply to Notre-Dame, though St-Eustache dates from a couple of hundred years later. The church is a curious architectural hybrid: With the exception of the feeble west front, added between 1754 and 1788, construction lasted from 1532 to 1637, spanning the decline of the Gothic style and the emergence of the Renaissance. *2 rue du Jour, tel. 01–46–27–89–21 for concert information. Daily 8–7. Métro: Les Halles; RER: Châtelet–Les Halles.*

㉝ ST-GERMAIN L'AUXERROIS. Until 1789 St-Germain was used by the French royal family as its parish church, in the days when the adjacent Louvre was a palace rather than a museum. The facade reveals the influence of 15th-century Flamboyant Gothic style, while the fluted columns around the choir, the area surrounding the altar, demonstrate the triumph of Classicism. *Pl. du Louvre. Métro: Louvre-Rivoli.*

26 ST-ROCH. Designed by Lemercier in 1653 but completed only in the 1730s, this huge church is almost as long as Notre-Dame (138 yards) thanks to Hardouin-Mansart's domed Lady Chapel at the far end. *Rue St-Honoré. Métro: Tuileries.*

THE GRANDS BOULEVARDS

An uninterrupted avenue runs in almost a straight line from St-Augustin, the city's grandest Second Empire church, to place de la République, whose very name symbolizes the ultimate downfall of the imperial regime. The avenue's name changes six times along the way, which is why Parisians refer to it as the *Grands Boulevards* (plural). The makeup of the neighborhoods along the Grand Boulevards changes steadily as you head east from the posh 8e arrondissement toward working-class east Paris. The *grands magasins* (department stores) at the start of the walk epitomize upscale Paris shopping. They stand on boulevard Haussmann, named in honor of the regional prefect who oversaw the reconstruction of the city in the 1850s and 1860s. The opulent Opéra Garnier, just past the grands magasins, is the architectural showpiece of the period (often termed the Second Empire and corresponding to the rule of Napoléon III).

Numbers in the margin correspond to the numbers on the Grands Boulevards map; these numbers indicate a suggested path for sightseeing.

Sights to See

40 BOURSE (Stock Exchange). The Paris Stock Exchange, a serene, colonnaded 19th-century building, is a far cry from Wall Street. Take your passport if you want to tour it. *Rue Vivienne. 30 frs. Guided tours only (in French), weekdays every ½ hr 1:15–3:45. Métro: Bourse.*

44 CIMETIÈRE DU PÈRE LACHAISE (Father Lachaise Cemetery). Cemeteries may not be your idea of the ultimate attraction, but this is the largest and most interesting in Paris. It forms a veritable necropolis, with cobbled avenues and tombs competing in

the grand boulevards

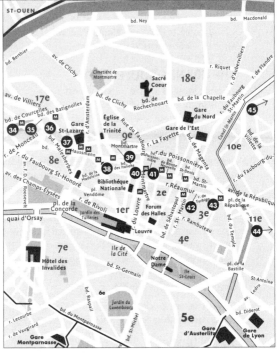

pomposity and originality. Leading incumbents include Jim Morrison, Frédéric Chopin, Marcel Proust, Edith Piaf, and Gertrude Stein. Get a map at the entrance and track them down. *Entrances on rue des Rondeaux, bd. de Ménilmontant, rue de la Réunion. Apr.–Sept., daily 8–6, Oct.–Mar., daily 8–5. Métro: Gambetta, Philippe-Auguste, Père Lachaise.*

39 HÔTEL DROUOT. Paris's central auction house has everything from stamps and toy soldiers to Renoirs and 18th-century commodes. The 16 salesrooms make for fascinating browsing, and there's no obligation to bid. *9 rue Drouot, tel. 01–48–00–20–00. Mid-Sept.–mid-July, viewings Mon.–Sat. 11–noon and 2–6, with auctions starting at 2. Métro: Richelieu-Drouot.*

35 MUSÉE CERNUSCHI. The collection includes Chinese art from Neolithic pottery (3rd century BC) to funeral statuary, painted 8th-century silks, and contemporary paintings, as well as ancient Persian bronze objects. *7 av. Velasquez, tel. 01–45–63–50–75. 17 frs. Tues.–Sun. 10–5:40. Métro: Monceau.*

36 MUSÉE NISSIM DE CAMONDO. The elegant decadence of the last days of the regal Ancien Régime is fully reflected in the lavish interior of this aristocratic Parisian mansion, built in the style of Louis XVI. *63 rue de Monceau, tel. 01–53–89–06–40. 30 frs. Wed.–Sun. 10–5. Métro: Villiers.*

41 NOTRE-DAME DE BONNE-NOUVELLE. This wide, soberly Neoclassical church, built 1823–29, is tucked away off the Grand Boulevards. *Rue de la Lune. Métro: Bonne-Nouvelle.*

★ **38 OPÉRA GARNIER.** The original Paris Opera, begun in 1862 by Charles Garnier at the behest of Napoléon III, was not completed until 1875, five years after the emperor's abdication. The ornate facade, cleaned 1999–2000, typifies Second Empire architecture: a pompous hodgepodge of styles, with all the subtlety of a Wagnerian cymbal crash. After paying the entrance fee, you can stroll around at leisure. The monumental foyer and staircase are impressive, and the stage is the largest in the world. Marc Chagall painted the ceiling in 1964. The **Musée de l'Opéra**, containing a few paintings and theatrical mementos, is unremarkable. *Pl. de l'Opéra, tel. 01–40–01–22–63. 30 frs, guided tours in English at 3 pm, 60 frs. Daily 10–5. Métro: Opéra.*

- -

NEED A BREAK?　Few cafés in Paris are grander than the Belle Epoque **Café de la Paix** (5 pl. de l'Opéra, tel. 01–40–07–30–10).

- -

34　PARC MONCEAU. The most picturesque gardens on the Right Bank were laid out as a private park in 1778 and retain some of the fanciful elements then in vogue, including mock ruins and a faux pyramid. *Entrances on bd. de Courcelles, av. Velasquez, av. Ruysdaël, av. van Dyck. Métro: Monceau.*

45　PARC DE LA VILLETTE. Usually known simply as La Villette, this ambitiously landscaped, futuristic park is home to the **Cité de la Musique** (☞ Nightlife and the Arts). This giant postmodern musical academy also houses the **Musée de la Musique** (Museum of Musical Instruments). At the **Géode** cinema, which looks like a huge silver golf ball, films are shown on an enormous 180-degree curved screen. The science museum, the **Cité des Sciences et de l'Industrie**, contains dozens of interactive exhibits (though most displays are in French only). *Science Museum: 30 av. Corentin-Cariou, tel. 01–40–05–80–00 for Science Museum. Museum of Musical Instruments 35 frs; Science Museum 35 frs. Museum of Musical Instruments Tues.–Sun. noon–6; Science Museum Tues.–Sun. 10–6. Métro: Porte de La Villette, Porte de Pantin.*

37　ST-AUGUSTIN. This domed church was dexterously constructed in the 1860s within the confines of an awkward V-shape site. It represented a breakthrough in ecclesiastical engineering because the use of metal pillars and girders obviated the need for exterior buttressing. *Pl. St-Augustin. Métro: St-Augustin.*

43 **STE-ÉLISABETH.** This studied essay in Baroque (1628–46) has brightly restored wall paintings and a wide, semicircular apse around the choir. *Rue du Temple. Métro: Temple.*

42 **ST-NICOLAS DES CHAMPS.** The rounded-arch, fluted Doric capitals in the chancel of this church date from 1560 to 1587, a full century later than the pointed-arch nave (1420–80). *Rue St-Martin. Métro: Arts-et-Métiers.*

THE MARAIS AND THE BASTILLE

The Marais is one of the city's most historic and sought-after residential districts. Except for the architecturally whimsical Pompidou Center, the tone here is set by the gracious architecture of the 17th and 18th centuries (the Marais was spared the attentions of Haussmann, the man who rebuilt so much of Paris in the mid-19th century). Today most of the Marais's spectacular *hôtels particuliers*—loosely translated as "mansions," the onetime residences of aristocratic families—have been restored; many are now museums, including the noted Musée Picasso. There are trendy boutiques and cafés among the kosher shops in what used to be a predominantly Jewish neighborhood around rue des Rosiers, and there's an impressive new Jewish Museum on nearby rue du Temple.

On the eastern edge of the Marais is place de la Bastille, site of the infamous prison stormed on July 14, 1789, an event that came to symbolize the beginning of the French Revolution. Largely in commemoration of the bicentennial of the Revolution, the Bastille area was renovated and became one of the trendiest sections of Paris. Galleries, shops, theaters, cafés, restaurants, and bars now fill formerly decrepit buildings and alleys.

Numbers in the margin correspond to the numbers on the Marais and the Bastille map; these numbers indicate a suggested path for sightseeing.

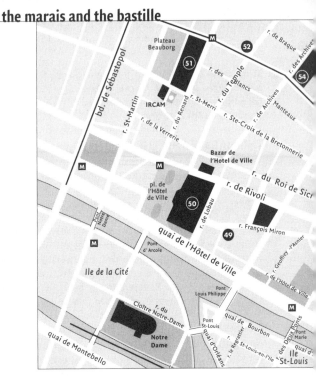

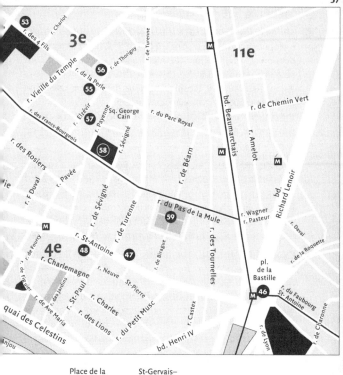

53

r. des 4 Fils

r. Charlot

3e

Vieille du Temple

r. de la Perle 56

55

r. de Thorigny

r. de Turenne

M

11e

r. de Chemin Vert

r. des Francs-Bourgeois

Elzévir

57 r. Payenne

Sq. George Cain

r. du Parc Royal

bd. Beaumarchais

r. Amelot

r. Sévigné

58

r. des Rosiers

r. F Duval

Pavée

r. de Sévigné

r. de Béarn

r. du Pas de la Mule

59

M

M

bd. Richard Lenoir

r. Daval

r. de Turenne

r. Wagner
r. Pasteur

r. de la Roquette

ie

M

4e 48

r. Charlemagne

r. St-Antoine

47

r. de Birague

r. des Tournelles

pl.
de la
Bastille

r. de Fourcy

r. Neuve
St-Pierre

r. des Jardins

de Fleur

r. St-Paul

r. Charles

r. des Lions

r. du Petit Musc

r. Castex

M 46

r. du Faubourg
St-Antoine

r. de Charonne

quai des Celestins

r. de Ave Maria

bd. Henri IV

r. de Lyon

Anjou

38

Sights to See

54 **ARCHIVES NATIONALES** (National Archives). If you're a serious history buff, you'll be fascinated by the thousands of historical documents, dating from the Merovingian period to the 20th century, at the National Archives. Architecture buffs will also enjoy this place, as it occupies the **Hôtel de Soubise,** one of the grandest of all Parisian mansions, whose salons were among the first to show the Rococo style in full bloom. *60 rue des Francs-Bourgeois, tel. 01–40–27–62–18. 20 frs. Mon. and Wed.–Fri. 10–5:45, weekends 1:45–5:45. Métro: Rambuteau.*

ATELIER BRANCUSI (Brancusi Studio). Romanian-born sculptor Constantin Brancusi settled in Paris in 1898 at age 22. This light, airy museum in front of the Pompidou Center contains four glass-fronted rooms that re-create Brancusi's studio, crammed with smooth, stylized works from all periods of his career. *11 rue St-Paul, tel. 01–44–78–12–33. 20 frs. Wed.–Mon. noon–10. Métro: Rambuteau.*

51 **CENTRE POMPIDOU.** The futuristic, funnel-top Pompidou Center—known to Parisians as Beaubourg, after the surrounding district—was built in the mid-1970s and named in honor of former French president Georges Pompidou (1911–74). After receiving many more visitors than intended over the years, the center was closed in 1997 for top-to-bottom renovation, reopening at the start of 2000. You approach the center across **place Georges-Pompidou,** a sloping piazza, home to the **Atelier Brancusi** (☞ *above*). The center is most famous for its **Musée National d'Art Moderne** (Modern Art Museum), recently extended to cover two stories: one devoted to figurative works from Fauvism and Cubism onward; the other to postwar abstract art and recent video-based creations. Also look for rotating exhibits of contemporary art. In addition, there are a public reference library, a language laboratory, an industrial design center, a cinema, a café, a rooftop restaurant, a gift shop, and the famous escalator that snakes up the outside to offer a sweeping panorama of central and western

Paris. Pl. Georges-Pompidou, tel. 01–44–78–12–33. 50 frs. Wed.–Mon. 11–10. Métro: Rambuteau.

47 **HÔTEL DE SULLY.** This late-Renaissance mansion, begun in 1624, has a stately garden and a majestic courtyard with statues, richly carved pediments, and dormer windows. It is the headquarters of the **Caisse Nationale des Monuments Historiques** (National Treasury of Historic Monuments), responsible for administering France's historic monuments. Guided visits to Paris sites and buildings begin here, though all are conducted in French. *62 rue St-Antoine, tel. 01–44–61–20–00. Métro: St-Paul.*

50 **HÔTEL DE VILLE** (City Hall). During the Commune of 1871, the Hôtel de Ville was burned to the ground. Today's building, based closely on the 16th-century Renaissance original, went up between 1874 and 1884. You can't inspect the lavish interior, but head around left to the traffic-free square, with its fountains and forest of street lamps, to admire the exuberant facade. *Pl. de l'Hôtel-de-Ville. Métro: Hôtel-de-Ville.*

52 **MUSÉE D'ART ET D'HISTOIRE DU JUDAÏSME** (Museum of Jewish Art and History). With its clifflike courtyard ringed by giant pilasters, Pierre Le Muet's Hôtel St-Aignan—completed 1650— is one of the most awesome sights in the Marais. It opened as a museum in 1998 after a 20-year, $35 million restoration. The interior has been remodeled to the point of blandness, but the displays—including silverware, clothing, and furniture—are carefully presented. *71 rue du Temple, tel. 01–53–01–86–53. 40 frs. Sun.–Fri. 11–6. Métro: Rambuteau.*

55 **MUSÉE BRICARD.** This museum—also called the Musée de la Serrure (Lock Museum)—is housed in a sober Baroque mansion designed in 1685 by the architect of Les Invalides, Libéral Bruand, for himself. If you've got a taste for fine craftsmanship, you will appreciate the intricacy and ingenuity of many of the locks displayed here. *1 rue de la Perle, tel. 01–42–77–79–62. 30 frs. Tues.– Fri. 10–noon and 2–5, Mon. 2–5. Métro: St-Paul.*

58 MUSÉE CARNAVALET. Two adjacent mansions in the heart of the Marais house the Carnavalet Museum, or the Paris History Museum, with material dating from the city's origins to the present. The museum is full of maps and plans, furniture, and busts and portraits of Parisian worthies down the ages. *23 rue de Sévigné, tel. 01–42–72–21–13. 27 frs. Tues.–Sun. 10–5:30. Métro: St-Paul.*

NEED A **Marais Plus** (20 rue des Francs-Bourgeois, tel. 01–48–87–01–
BREAK? 40), on the corner of rue Elzévir and rue des Francs-Bourgeois, is a delightful, artsy gift shop with a cozy *salon de thé* at the rear.

---

53 MUSÉE DE LA CHASSE ET DE LA NATURE (Museum of Hunting and Nature). This museum is housed in the Hôtel de Guénégaud, designed around 1650 by François Mansart. There is a series of immense 17th- and 18th-century still lifes (notably by Desportes and Oudry) and a wide variety of swords, guns, muskets, and taxidermy. *60 rue des Archives, tel. 01–42–72–86–42. 30 frs. Wed.–Mon. 11–6. Métro: Rambuteau.*

57 MUSÉE COGNACQ-JAY. Prized by connoisseurs, this museum is devoted to the arts of the 18th century and contains outstanding furniture, porcelain, and paintings (notably by Watteau, Boucher, and Tiepolo). *8 rue Elzévir, tel. 01–40–27–07–21. 22 frs. Tues.–Sun. 10–5:40. Métro: St-Paul.*

★ **56 MUSÉE PICASSO.** Housed in the 17th-century Hôtel Salé, this museum contains the paintings, sculptures, drawings, prints, ceramics, and assorted works of art given to the government by Picasso's heirs after the painter's death in 1973 in lieu of death duties. There are works from every period of Picasso's life, as well as pieces by Cézanne, Miró, Renoir, Braque, Degas, and Matisse. *5 rue de Thorigny, tel. 01–42–71–25–21. 30 frs, Sun. 20 frs. Wed.–Mon. 9:30–5:30. Métro: St-Sébastien.*

OPÉRA DE LA BASTILLE. The state-of-the-art Bastille Opera was erected on the south side of place de la Bastille. Designed by

Argentine-born Carlos Ott, it opened on July 14, 1989, in commemoration of the bicentennial of the French Revolution. The steep-climbing auditorium seats more than 3,000 and has earned more plaudits than the curving glass facade. *Pl. de la Bastille, tel. 01–40–01–19–70. Guided tours 50 frs. Métro: Bastille.*

46 PLACE DE LA BASTILLE. Nothing remains of the infamous Bastille prison destroyed at the beginning of the French Revolution. In the midst of the large traffic circle is the **Colonne de Juillet** (July Column), commemorating the overthrow of Charles X in July 1830. As part of the countrywide celebrations for July 1989, the bicentennial of the French Revolution, the Opéra de la Bastille (☞ *above*) was erected, inspiring substantial redevelopment on the surrounding streets, especially along rue de Lappe and rue de la Roquette. What was formerly a humdrum neighborhood rapidly gained art galleries, clubs, and bars. *Métro: Bastille.*

★ **59 PLACE DES VOSGES.** Laid out by Henri IV at the start of the 17th century and originally known as place Royale, this square is the oldest and one of the prettiest in Paris. The two larger buildings on either side were originally the king's and queen's pavilions. The statue in the center is of Louis XIII. At No. 6 is the **Maison de Victor Hugo** (Victor Hugo's home), where the workaholic French author, famed for *Les Misérables* and *The Hunchback of Notre-Dame*, lived between 1832 and 1848. *Maison de Victor Hugo: 6 pl. des Vosges, tel. 01–42–72–10–16. 27 frs. Tues.–Sun. 10–5:45. Métro: St-Paul, Chemin-Vert.*

49 ST-GERVAIS–ST-PROTAIS. This imposing church near the Hôtel de Ville is named after two Roman soldiers martyred by the emperor Nero in the 1st century AD. The church, a riot of Flamboyant style, went up between 1494 and 1598, making it one of the last Gothic constructions in the country. The facade, constructed between 1616 and 1621, is an early example of French use of classical decoration on the capitals (topmost sections) of the columns. *Pl. St-Gervais, tel. 01–47–26–78–38 for concert information. Tues.–Sun. 6:30 am–8 pm. Métro: Hôtel-de-Ville.*

48 ST-PAUL–ST-LOUIS. The leading Baroque church in the Marais, with its elegant dome soaring 180 ft above the crossing, was begun in 1627 by the Jesuits and partly modeled on their Gesu church in Rome. Look for Delacroix's dramatic *Christ on the Mount of Olives* high up in the transept. *Rue St-Antoine. Métro: St-Paul.*

THE ILE ST-LOUIS AND THE LATIN QUARTER

Set behind the Ile de la Cité is one of the most romantic corners of Paris—tiny Ile St-Louis, where clocks seem to have been stopped sometime in the 19th century. South of the Ile St-Louis on the Left Bank of the Seine is the bohemian Quartier Latin (Latin Quarter), with its warren of steep, sloping streets, populated largely by Sorbonne students and academics. The name *Latin Quarter* comes from the old university tradition of studying and speaking in Latin, a tradition that disappeared during the Revolution. The university began as a theological school in the Middle Ages and later became the headquarters of the University of Paris; in 1968 the student revolution here had an explosive effect on French politics, resulting in major reforms in the education system. Most of the district's appeal is less emphatic: Roman ruins, tumbling street markets, the two oldest trees in Paris, and chance glimpses of Notre-Dame all await your discovery.

Numbers in the margin correspond to the numbers on the Ile St-Louis and the Latin Quarter map; these numbers indicate a suggested path for sightseeing.

Sights to See

👌 **67 ARÈNES DE LUTÈCE** (Lutetia Amphitheater). This Roman arena was only discovered in 1869 and has since been excavated and landscaped to reveal parts of the original amphitheater. Designed as a theater and circus, the arena was almost totally destroyed by the Barbarians in AD 280, although you can still see part of the stage and tiered seating. *Entrances on rue Monge and rue de Navarre. Daily 8–sunset. Métro: Monge.*

60 ILE ST-LOUIS. One of the more fabled addresses in Paris, this tiny island has long harbored the rich and famous, including Chopin, Helena Rubenstein, Chagall, and the Rothschild family, which still occupies the island's grandest house, the Hôtel Lambert, which is set on the eastern prow of the island. In fact, the entire island displays striking architectural unity, stemming from the efforts of a group of early 17th-century property speculators led by Christophe Marie. The group commissioned leading Baroque architect Louis Le Vau (1612–70) to erect a series of imposing town houses. Other than some elegant facades and the island's highly picturesque quays along the Seine, there are no major sights here—just follow your nose and soak in the atmosphere of old Paris. *Métro: Pont-Marie.*

NEED A BREAK? Cafés all over sell Berthillon, the haute couture of ice cream, but the **Berthillon** (31 rue St-Louis-en-l'Ile, tel. 01–43–54–31–61) shop itself is the place to come. More than 30 flavors are served; expect to wait in line. The shop is open Wednesday–Sunday.

68 INSTITUT DU MONDE ARABE (Institute of the Arab World). Jean Nouvel's striking 1988 glass-and-steel edifice adroitly fuses Arabic and European styles. Note the 240 shutterlike apertures that open and close to regulate light exposure. Inside, the institute tries to do for Arab culture what the Pompidou Center does for modern art, with the help of a sound-and-image center, a vast library and documentation center, and an art museum. The top-floor café provides a good view of Paris. *1 rue des Fossés-St-Bernard, tel. 01–40–51–38–38. 25 frs. Tues.–Sun. 10–6. Métro: Cardinal-Lemoine.*

66 JARDIN DES PLANTES (Botanical Garden). This enormous swath of greenery contains the botanical garden, the Grande Galerie de l'Évolution, and three natural history museums: the **Musée Entomologique** (15-franc admission), devoted to insects; the **Musée Paléontologique** (30-franc admission), to fossils and prehistoric animals; and the **Musée Minéralogique** (30-franc

the ile st-louis and the latin quarter

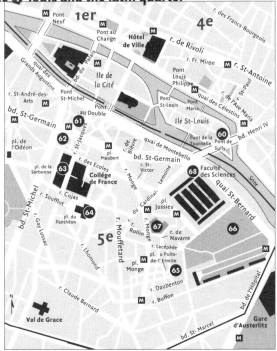

admission), to rocks and minerals. It also has an alpine garden, an aquarium, a maze, a number of hothouses (15-franc admission), and one of the world's oldest zoos. *Entrances on rue Geoffroy-St-Hilaire, rue Cuvier and rue Buffon. Zoo 30 frs. Garden daily 7:30–sunset; zoo daily 9–6; museums Wed.–Mon. 10–5. Métro: Monge, Jussieu, Gare d'Austerlitz.*

65 MOSQUÉE (Mosque). The city mosque was built from 1922 to 1925, complete with arcades and minaret, and decorated in the style of Moorish Spain. The sunken garden and tiled patios are open to the public (the prayer rooms are not) and so are the *hammams*, or Turkish baths. Venture in and sip a restorative cup of sweet mint tea at the café. *2 pl. du Puits-de-l'Ermite, tel. 01–45–35–97–33. 15 frs guided tour, 85 frs Turkish baths. Baths daily 10 am–9 pm; Tues. and Sun. men only; Mon. and Wed.–Sat. women only. Guided tours of mosque Sat.–Thurs. 9–noon and 2–6. Métro: Monge.*

★ **62 MUSÉE NATIONAL DU MOYEN-AGE** (National Museum of the Middle Ages). This museum is housed in the famous 15th-century Hôtel de Cluny. The mansion has an intricately vaulted chapel and a cloistered courtyard with mullioned windows that originally belonged to monks of the Cluny Abbey in Burgundy, hence the museum's former name, the Musée de Cluny. A stunning array of tapestries heads its vast exhibition of medieval decorative arts. Alongside the mansion are the city's Roman baths and the *Boatmen's Pillar*, Paris's oldest sculpture. *6 pl. Paul-Painlevé, tel. 01–53–73–78–00. 30 frs, Sun. 20 frs. Wed.–Mon. 9:15–5:45. Métro: Cluny–La Sorbonne.*

64 PANTHÉON. Originally commissioned as a church by Louis XV as a mark of gratitude for his recovery from a grave illness in 1744, the Panthéon is now a monument to France's most glorious historical figures, including Voltaire, Zola, Rousseau, and dozens of French statesmen, military heroes, and other thinkers. Germain Soufflot's building was not begun until 1764; nor completed until 1790, during the French Revolution, whereupon its windows were blocked and it was transformed into the national shrine it is today.

A giant pendulum, suspended on a 220-ft steel wire, commemorates Léon Foucault's 1851 experiment to prove the earth's rotation. *Pl. du Panthéon, tel. 01–44–32–18–00. 35 frs. Summer, daily 9:30–6:30; winter, daily 10–6:15. Métro: Cardinal-Lemoine; RER: Luxembourg.*

61 ST-SÉVERIN. This unusually wide, Flamboyant Gothic church dominates a Left Bank neighborhood filled with squares and pedestrian streets. Note the splendidly deviant spiraling column in the forest of pillars behind the altar. *Rue des Prêtres St-Séverin. Weekdays 11–5:30, Sat. 11–10. Métro: St-Michel.*

63 SORBONNE. Named after Robert de Sorbon, a medieval canon who founded a theological college here in 1253, this is one of the oldest universities in Europe. The church and university buildings were restored by Cardinal Richelieu in the 17th century, and the maze of amphitheaters, lecture rooms, and laboratories, along with the surrounding courtyards and narrow streets, retains a hallowed air. You can visit the main courtyard on rue de la Sorbonne and peek into the main lecture hall, a major meeting point during the tumultuous student upheavals of 1968. The square is dominated by the noble university church with cupola and Corinthian columns. Inside is the white-marble tomb of that ultimate crafty cleric, Cardinal Richelieu himself. *Rue de la Sorbonne. Métro: Cluny–La Sorbonne.*

FROM ORSAY TO ST-GERMAIN

This walk covers the Left Bank, from the Musée d'Orsay in the stately 7e arrondissement to the lively and colorful area around St-Germain-des-Prés in the 6e. The Musée d'Orsay, in a daringly converted Belle Epoque rail station on the Seine, houses one of the world's most spectacular arrays of Impressionist paintings. Farther along the river, the 18th-century Palais Bourbon, home to the National Assembly, sets the tone for the 7e arrondissement. Luxurious ministries and embassies—including the Hôtel Matignon, residence of the French prime minister—line the surrounding streets, their majestic scale in total keeping with the

Hôtel des Invalides, whose gold-leafed dome climbs heavenward above the regal tomb of Napoléon. The Rodin Museum—set in one of the city's prettiest mansions—is only a short walk away.

To the east, away from the splendor of the 7ᵉ, the boulevard St-Michel slices the Left Bank in two: on one side, the Latin Quarter (☞ The Ile St-Louis and the Latin Quarter, *above*); on the other, the Faubourg St-Germain, named for St-Germain-des-Prés, the oldest church in Paris. The venerable church tower has long acted as a beacon for intellectuals, most famously during the 1950s when Albert Camus, Jean-Paul Sartre, and Simone de Beauvoir ate and drank existentialism in the neighborhood cafés. Today most of the philosophizing is done by tourists, yet a wealth of bookshops, art stores, and antiques galleries ensure that St-Germain, as the area is commonly known, retains its highbrow appeal. In the southern part of this district is the city's most famous and colorful park, the Jardin du Luxembourg.

Numbers in the margin correspond to the numbers on the Orsay to St-Germain map; these numbers indicate a suggested path for sightseeing.

Sights to See

76 ATELIER DELACROIX (Delacroix's Studio). The studio of artist Eugène Delacroix (1798–1863) contains only a small collection of his sketches and drawings. But if you want to pay homage to France's foremost Romantic painter, you'll want to visit this museum. Speaking of pictures, don't forget to take some photographs here of place Furstenberg, one of the loveliest corners of 19th-century Paris still extant. *6 rue Furstenberg, tel. 01–44–41–86–50. 22 frs. Wed.–Mon. 9:30–5. Métro: St-Germain-des-Prés.*

77 ÉCOLE NATIONALE DES BEAUX-ARTS (National Fine Arts College). In three large mansions near the Seine, this school—today the breeding ground for painters, sculptors, and architects—was once the site of a convent, founded in 1608. Wander into the courtyard and galleries of the school to see the casts and copies

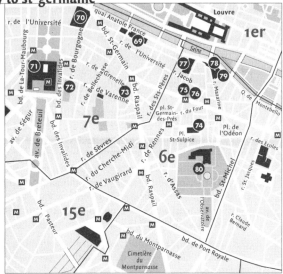

of the statues stored here for safekeeping during the Revolution.
14 rue Bonaparte. Daily 1–7. Métro: St-Germain-des-Prés.

NEED A
BREAK?
The popular **La Palette** café (43 rue de Seine, tel. 01–43–26–68–
15), on the corner of rue de Seine and rue Callot, has long been
a favorite haunt of Beaux-Arts students.

★ **71** **HÔTEL DES INVALIDES.** Les Invalides, as it is widely known, is an outstanding monumental Baroque ensemble, designed by Libéral Bruand in the 1670s at the behest of Louis XIV to house wounded, or *invalid*, soldiers. Although no more than a handful of old-timers live at the Invalides these days, the army link remains in the form of the **Musée de l'Armée,** a military museum. The **Musée des Plans-Reliefs,** also housed here, contains a fascinating collection of old scale models of French towns. The 17th-century **Église St-Louis des Invalides** is the Invalides' original church. More impressive is Jules Hardouin-Mansart's **Église du Dôme,** built onto the end of the church of St-Louis but blocked off from it in 1793. The showpiece is Napoléon's grandiose tomb. *Pl. des Invalides, tel. 01–44–42–37–72. 38 frs. Apr.–Sept., daily 10–5:45; Oct.–Mar., daily 10–4:45. Métro: Latour-Maubourg.*

79 **HÔTEL DE LA MONNAIE** (Mint). Louis XVI transferred the Royal Mint to this imposing mansion in the late 18th century. Although the mint was moved again, to Pessac, near Bordeaux, in 1973, weights and measures, medals, and limited-edition coins are still made here. The **Musée de la Monnaie** (Coin Museum) has an extensive collection of coins, documents, and engravings, plus a good shop. On Tuesday and Friday at 2 you can catch the coin metal craftsmen at work. *11 quai de Conti, tel. 01–40–46–55–35. 20 frs. Tues.–Fri. 11–5:30, weekends noon–5:30. Métro: Pont-Neuf.*

78 **INSTITUT DE FRANCE** (French Institute). Built to the designs of Louis Le Vau from 1662 to 1674, the institute's curved, dome-top facade is one of the Left Bank's most impressive waterside sights. It also houses one of France's most revered cultural institutions, the Académie Française, created by Cardinal Richelieu in 1635. The interior, unfortunately, is closed to the public. *Pl. de l'Institut. Métro: Pont-Neuf.*

🐦 **80** **JARDIN DU LUXEMBOURG** (Luxembourg Gardens). One of the prettiest of Paris's few large parks, the Luxembourg Gardens have fountains, ponds, trim hedges, precisely planted rows of trees, and gravel walks typical of the French fondness for formal landscaping.

The 17th-century **Palais de Luxembourg** (Luxembourg Palace), overlooking the gardens, houses the French Senate and is not open to the public. It was built, like the gardens, for Maria de' Medici, widow of Henri IV. *Métro: Odéon; RER: Luxembourg.*

73 **MUSÉE MAILLOL.** Drawings, paintings, tapestries, and, above all, bronzes by Art Deco sculptor Aristide Maillol (1861–1944)—whose sleek, stylized nudes adorn the Tuileries—can be admired at this handsome town house, lovingly restored by his former muse Dina Vierny. *61 rue de Grenelle, tel. 01–42–22–59–58. 40 frs. Wed.–Mon. 11–6. Métro: Rue du Bac.*

★ **69** **MUSÉE D'ORSAY.** In a stylishly converted train station, the Orsay Museum—devoted to the arts (mainly French) spanning the period 1848–1914—is one of the city's most popular. The main artistic attraction is the Impressionists: Renoir, Sisley, Pissarro, and Monet are all well represented. The post-Impressionists—Cézanne, van Gogh, Gauguin, and Toulouse-Lautrec—are on the top floor. On the ground floor you'll find the work of Manet, the powerful realism of Courbet, and the delicate nuances of Degas. If you prefer more academic paintings, look for Puvis de Chavannes's larger-than-life classical canvases. And if you're excited by more modern developments, look for the early 20th-century Fauves (meaning "wild beasts," the name given them by an outraged critic in 1905)—particularly Matisse, Derain, and Vlaminck. Thought-provoking sculptures also lurk at every turn. *1 rue de Bellechasse, tel. 01–40–49–48–84. 40 frs, Sun. 30 frs. Tues.–Wed. and Fri.–Sat. 10–6, Thurs. 10–9:45, Sun. 9–6. Métro: Solférino; RER: Musée d'Orsay.*

NEED A BREAK? Find respite from the overwhelming collection of art in the **Musée d'Orsay Café** behind one of the giant station clocks, close to the Impressionist galleries on the top floor.

★ **72** **MUSÉE RODIN.** The exquisite 18th-century Hôtel Biron makes a gracious setting for the sculpture of Auguste Rodin (1840–1917).

You'll doubtless recognize the seated *Le Penseur* (*The Thinker*), with his elbow resting on his knee, and the passionate *Le Baiser* (*The Kiss*). From the upper rooms, which contain some fine if murky paintings by Rodin's friend Eugène Carrière (1849–1906) and some fine sculptures by Rodin's mistress, Camille Claudel (1864–1943), you can see the large garden behind the house. Don't skip the garden: It is exceptional both for its rosebushes (more than 2,000 of them) and for its sculpture. *77 rue de Varenne, tel. 01–44–18–61–10. 28 frs, Sun. 18 frs; gardens only 5 frs. Easter–Oct., Tues.–Sun. 9:30–5:45; Nov.–Easter, Tues.–Sun. 9:30–4:45. Métro: Varenne.*

70 **PALAIS BOURBON.** The most prominent feature of the home of the Assemblée Nationale (French Parliament) is its colonnaded facade, commissioned by Napoléon. *Pl. du Palais-Bourbon. During temporary exhibits only. Métro: Assemblée Nationale.*

75 **ST-GERMAIN-DES-PRÉS.** Paris's oldest church was first built to shelter a relic of the true cross, brought back from Spain in AD 542. The chancel was enlarged and the church then consecrated by Pope Alexander III in 1163; the tall, sturdy tower—a Left Bank landmark—dates from this period. The church stages superb organ concerts and recitals. *Pl. St-Germain. Weekdays 8–7:30, weekends 8–9. Métro: St-Germain-des-Prés.*

74 **ST-SULPICE.** Dubbed the "Cathedral of the Left Bank," this enormous 17th-century church is of note for the powerful Delacroix frescoes in the first chapel on the right. The 18th-century facade was never finished, and its unequal towers add a playful touch to an otherwise sober design. *Pl. St-Sulpice. Métro: St-Sulpice.*

MONTPARNASSE

One and one-half kilometers (1 mile) south of the Seine is the district of Montparnasse, named after Mount Parnassus, the Greek mountain associated with the worship of Apollo and the Muses. Montparnasse's cultural heyday came in the first four decades of the 20th century, when it replaced Montmartre as the place for painters and poets to live, which prompted the launch of a string of artsy brasseries along the district's main thoroughfare, the broad boulevard du Montparnasse. The boulevard may lack poetic charm these days, but nightlife stays the pace, as bars, clubs, restaurants, and cinemas crackle with energy beneath Europe's second-tallest high-rise: the 59-story Tour Montparnasse. Although the tower itself is a typically bland product of the early 1970s, of note only for the view from the top, several more-adventurous buildings have risen in its wake: Ricardo Boffil's semicircular Amphithéâtre housing complex, the glass-cubed Cartier Center for Contemporary Art, and the Montparnasse train station with its giant glass facade and designer garden above the tracks. If you have a deeper feel for history, you may prefer the Baroque church of Val-de-Grâce or the quiet Montparnasse Cemetery.

Numbers in the margin correspond to the numbers on the Montparnasse map; these numbers indicate a suggested path for sightseeing.

Sights to See

84 CIMETIÈRE DU MONTPARNASSE (Montparnasse Cemetery). This cemetery is not picturesque, but it contains many of the quarter's most illustrious residents: Charles Baudelaire, Auguste Bartholdi, Jean-Paul Sartre, Man Ray, Samuel Beckett, Jean Seberg, and Serge Gainsbourg. *Entrances at rue Froidevaux, bd. Edgar-Quinet. Métro: Raspail, Gaîté.*

85 FONDATION CARTIER (Cartier Foundation). Architect Jean Nouvel's eye-catching giant glass cubicle is a suitable setting for the temporary, thought-provoking shows of contemporary art organized here by jewelry giant Cartier. *261 bd. Raspail, tel. 01–42–18–56–50. 30 frs. Tues.–Sun. noon–8. Métro: Raspail.*

82 JARDIN ATLANTIQUE (Atlantic Garden). This small park, which opened in 1994, was planted on a concourse constructed over the first 100 yards of the tracks leading to the Gare Montparnasse. It

ONE LAST TRAVEL TIP:

Pack an easy way to reach the world.

Wherever you travel, the MCI WorldCom Card℠ is the easiest way to stay in touch. You can use it to call to and from more than 125 countries worldwide. And you can earn bonus miles every time you use your card. So go ahead, travel the world. MCI WorldCom℠ makes it even more rewarding. For additional access codes, visit **www.wcom.com/worldphone**.

MCI WORLDCOM.

EASY TO CALL WORLDWIDE

1. Just dial the WorldPhone® access number of the country you're calling from.

2. Dial or give the operator your MCI WorldCom Card number.

3. Dial or give the number you're calling.

Belgium ◆	0800-10012
Czech Republic ◆	00-42-000112
Denmark ◆	8001-0022

France ◆	0-800-99-0019
Germany	0800-888-8000
Hungary ◆	06▼-800-01411
Ireland	1-800-55-1001
Italy ◆	172-1022
Mexico	01-800-021-8000
Netherlands ◆	0800-022-91-22
Spain	900-99-0014
Switzerland ◆	0800-89-0222
United Kingdom	0800-89-0222
United States	1-800-888-8000

◆ Public phones may require deposit of coin or phone card for dial tone.　▼ Wait for second dial tone.

EARN FREQUENT FLIER MILES

Bureau de change

Cambio

外国為替

In this city, you can find money on almost any street.

NO-FEE FOREIGN EXCHANGE

The Chase Manhattan Bank has over 80 convenient locations near New York City destinations such as:

Times Square
Rockefeller Center
Empire State Building
2 World Trade Center
United Nations Plaza

Exchange any of 75 foreign currencies

 CHASE

THE RIGHT RELATIONSHIP IS EVERYTHING.®

features an assortment of trees and plants from countries on the Atlantic Ocean. What looks like a quirky metal sculpture in the middle of the park is, in fact, a weather observatory with a battery of flickering lights charting temperature, wind speed, and rainfall. *Pont des Cinq-Martyrs-du-Lycée-Buffon. Métro: Montparnasse-Bienvenüe.*

83 **PLACE DE CATALOGNE.** This square is dominated by Ricardo Boffil's monumental **Amphithéâtre** housing complex, with its chunky reinvention of classical detail. Just behind is the turn-of-the-century church of **Notre-Dame du Travail,** whose riveted iron-and-steel framework was meant to symbolize the work ethos enshrouded in the church's name. *Métro: Gaîté.*

81 **TOUR MONTPARNASSE** (Montparnasse Tower). As Europe's second-tallest skyscraper, completed in 1973, this 685-ft tower offers a stupendous view of Paris from its open-air roof terrace. Fifty-two of the 59 stories are taken up by offices and a vast commercial complex, including a Galeries Lafayette department store, spreads over the first floor. Banal by day, the tower becomes Montparnasse's neon-lighted beacon at night. **Place du 18-Juin-1940,** beneath Tour Montparnasse, is named for the date of the radio speech Charles de Gaulle broadcast from London, urging the French to resist the Germans after the Nazi invasion of May 1940. It was here that German military governor Dietrich von Choltitz surrendered to the Allies in August 1944, ignoring Hitler's orders to destroy the city as he withdrew. A plaque on the wall commemorates the event. *Rue de l'Arrivée, tel. 01–45–38–52–56. 46 frs. Apr.–Sept., daily 9:30 am–11:30 pm; Oct.–Mar., daily 9:30 am–10:30 pm. Métro: Montparnasse-Bienvenüe.*

86 **VAL DE GRÂCE.** This imposing 17th-century Left Bank church was commissioned by Anne of Austria and designed by François Mansart. Its powerfully rhythmic two-story facade rivals the Dôme Church at the Invalides as the city's most striking example of Italianate Baroque. *1 Pl. Alphonse-Laveran. RER: Port-Royal.*

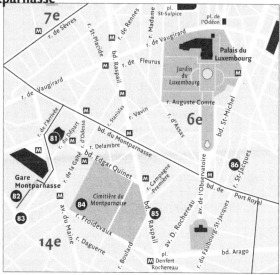

MONTMARTRE

On a dramatic rise above the city is Montmartre, site of the Sacré-Coeur Basilica and home to a once-thriving artistic community. Although the fabled nightlife of old Montmartre has fizzled down to some glitzy nightclubs and porn shows, Montmartre still exudes history and Gallic charm. Windmills once dotted Montmartre (often referred to by Parisians as *La Butte*, meaning "mound"). They were set up here not just because the hill was a good place to catch the wind—at more than 300 ft, it's the highest point in the city—but because Montmartre was covered with wheat fields and quarries right up to the end of the 19th century. Today only two of the original 20 windmills remain. Visiting Montmartre means negotiating a lot of steep streets and flights of steps. The crown atop this urban peak, the Sacré-Coeur Basilica, is something of an architectural oddity. It has been called everything from grotesque to sublime; its silhouette, viewed from afar at dusk or sunrise, looks more like a mosque than a cathedral.

Numbers in the margin correspond to the numbers on the Montmartre map; these numbers indicate a suggested path for sightseeing.

Sights to See

🕤 **BATEAU-LAVOIR** (Boat Wash House). Montmartre poet Max Jacob coined the name for the original building on this site (which burned down in 1970), saying it resembled a boat and that the warren of artists' studios within was perpetually paint-splattered and in need of a good hosing down. It was here that Pablo Picasso and Georges Braque made their first bold stabs at the concept of Cubism. The new building also contains art studios, but is the epitome of poured-concrete drabness. *13 pl. Émile-Goudeau. Métro: Abbesses.*

🕤 **ESPACE DALÍ** (Dalí Center). Some of Salvador Dalí's less familiar works are among the 25 sculptures and 300 prints housed in this museum with an atmosphere that is meant to approximate the surreal experience. *11 rue Poulbot, tel. 01–42–64–40–10. 40 frs. Daily 10–6:30. Métro: Abbesses.*

🕤 **LAPIN AGILE.** This bar-cabaret, originally one of the raunchiest haunts in Montmartre, got its curious name—the Nimble Rabbit—when the owner, André Gill, hung up a sign of a laughing rabbit jumping out of a saucepan clutching a bottle of wine. Locals christened it the *Lapin à Gill*, meaning "Gill's rabbit." When, in 1886, it was sold to cabaret singer Jules Jouy, he called it the Lapin Agile, a French homonym of "Lapin à Gill." In 1903 the premises were bought by the most celebrated cabaret entrepreneur of them all, Aristide Bruand, depicted by Toulouse-Lautrec in a

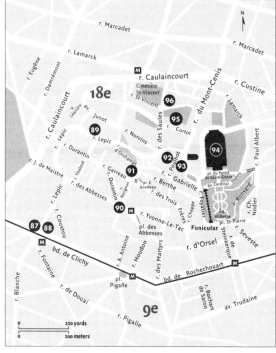

series of famous posters. *22 rue des Saules, tel. 01–46–06–85–87. 130 frs. Tues.–Sat. 9 pm–2 am. Métro: Lamarck-Caulaincourt.*

89 **MOULIN DE LA GALETTE** (Biscuit Windmill). This is one of two remaining windmills in Montmartre. It was once the focal point of an open-air cabaret (made famous in a painting by Renoir). Rumor has it that in 1814 the miller Debray, who had struggled in vain to defend the windmill from invading Cossacks, was then strung up on its sails and spun to death by the invaders. Unfortunately, it is privately owned and can only be admired from the street below. *Rue Tholozé. Métro: Abbesses.*

87 **MOULIN ROUGE** (Red Windmill). This world-famous cabaret was built in 1885 as a windmill, then transformed into a dance hall in 1900. Those wild, early days were immortalized by Toulouse-Lautrec in his posters and paintings. It still trades shamelessly on the notion of Paris as a city of sin: If you fancy a Vegas-style night out, this is the place to go. *82 bd. de Clichy, tel. 01–53–09–82–82. 360–550 frs. Shows nightly at 9 and 11. Métro: Blanche.*

88 **MUSÉE DE L'EROTISME** (Erotic Art Museum). Opened in 1997, this museum claims to offer "a prestigious showcase for every kind of erotic fantasy." Its 2,000 works of art—some might question that term—range from Peruvian potteries, African carvings, and Indian miniatures to Nepalese bronzes, Chinese ivories, and Japanese prints. *72 bd. de Clichy, tel. 01–42–58–28–73. 40 frs. Daily 10 am–2 am. Métro: Blanche.*

95 **MUSÉE DE MONTMARTRE** (Montmartre Museum). In its turn-of-the-century heyday, Montmartre's historical museum was home to an illustrious group of painters, writers, and assorted cabaret artists. Foremost among them were Renoir and Maurice Utrillo. The museum also provides a view of the tiny **vineyard**—the only one in Paris—on neighboring rue des Saules. A token 125 gallons of wine are still produced every year. *12 rue Cortot, tel. 01–46–06–61–11. 25 frs. Tues.–Sun. 11–6. Métro: Lamarck-Caulaincourt.*

90 PLACE DES ABBESSES. This triangular square is typical of the picturesque, slightly countrified style that has made Montmartre famous. The entrance to the Abbesses métro station, a curving, sensuous mass of delicate iron, is one of only two original Art Nouveau entrance canopies left in Paris. *Métro: Abbesses.*

93 PLACE DU TERTRE. This tumbling square (*tertre* means "hillock") regains its village atmosphere only in the winter, when the branches of the plane trees sketch traceries against the sky. At any other time of year you'll be confronted by crowds of tourists and a swarm of third-rate artists clamoring to do your portrait (if one of them produces an unsolicited portrait, you are not obligated to buy it). **La Mère Catherine,** on one corner of the square, was a favorite with the Russian Cossacks who occupied Paris in 1814. They couldn't have suspected that, by banging on the table and yelling "bistro" (Russian for "quickly"), they were inventing a new breed of French restaurant. *Métro: Abbesses.*

NEED A BREAK? **Patachou** (9 pl. du Tertre, tel. 01–42–51–06–06), serving exquisite if expensive cakes and teas, sounds the one classy note on place du Tertre.

94 SACRÉ-COEUR. The Sacred Heart Basilica was erected as a sort of national guilt offering in expiation for the blood shed during the Paris Commune and Franco-Prussian War in 1870–71 and was largely financed by French Catholics fearful of an anticlerical backlash under the new republican regime. The basilica was not consecrated until 1919. Stylistically, the Sacré-Coeur borrows elements from Romanesque and Byzantine models. The gloomy, cavernous interior is worth visiting for its golden mosaics; climb to the top of the dome for the view of Paris. *Pl. du Parvis-du-Sacré-Coeur. Métro: Anvers.*

Distance Conversion Chart

Kilometers/Miles

To change kilometers (km) to miles (mi), multiply km by .621.
To change mi to km, multiply mi by 1.61.

km to mi	mi to km
1 = .62	1 = 1.6
2 = 1.2	2 = 3.2
3 = 1.9	3 = 4.8
4 = 2.5	4 = 6.4
5 = 3.1	5 = 8.1
6 = 3.7	6 = 9.7
7 = 4.3	7 = 11.3
8 = 5.0	8 = 12.9

Meters/Feet

To change meters (m) to feet (ft), multiply m by 3.28.
To change ft to m, multiply ft by .305.

m to ft	ft to m
1 = 3.3	1 = .30
2 = 6.6	2 = .61
3 = 9.8	3 = .92
4 = 13.1	4 = 1.2
5 = 16.4	5 = 1.5
6 = 19.7	6 = 1.8
7 = 23.0	7 = 2.1
8 = 26.2	8 = 2.4

In This Section

Revised and updated by Alexander Lobrano
and Brandy Whittingham

eating out

WHETHER YOU GET KNEE-DEEP in white truffles at Les Ambassadeurs or merely discover pistachioed sausage (the poor man's caviar) at a classic corner bistro, you'll discover that food in Paris is an obsession, an art, a subject of endless debate. From the edible genius of haute cuisine wizard Alain Ducasse—whose turbot with "marmalade" of asparagus will make you purr—to brilliant bistro chef Yves Camdeborde's red mullet with chestnuts and cèpes, dining in Paris can easily leave you in a pleasurable stupor. And when it all seems a bit overwhelming, you can slip away to a casual little place for an earthy, bubbling cassoulet, have a midnight feast of the world's silkiest oysters, or even opt out of Gaul altogether for superb pasta, couscous, or an herb-bright Vietnamese stir-fry. Once you know where to go, Paris is a city where perfection awaits at all levels of the food chain.

Generally, restaurants are open from noon to about 2 and from 7:30 or 8 to 10 or 10:30. It's best to make reservations, particularly in summer, although the reviews only state when reservations are absolutely essential. If you want no-smoking seating, make this clear; the mandatory no-smoking area is sometimes limited to a very few tables. Brasseries have longer hours and often serve all day and late into the evening; some are open 24 hours. Assume a restaurant is open every day unless otherwise indicated. Surprisingly, many prestigious restaurants close on Saturday as well as Sunday. July and August are the most common months for annual closings, although Paris in August is no longer the wasteland it once was. Although prices include tax and tip by law, pocket change left on the table in simple places, or an additional 5% in better restaurants, is appreciated. Places where a jacket and tie are de rigueur are noted. Otherwise, use common sense—jeans and T-shirts are not suitable in Paris restaurants, nor are shorts or running clothes, except in the most casual bistros and cafés.

CATEGORY	COST*
$$$$	over 550 frs
$$$	300 frs–550 frs
$$	175 frs–300 frs
$	under 175 frs

*per person for a three-course meal, including 20.6% tax and service but not drinks

RESTAURANTS
1er Arrondissement (Louvre/Les Halles)

FRENCH

$$$$ **LE GRAND VÉFOUR.** Victor Hugo could stride in and still recognize
★ this place—then, as now, a contender for the prize for the most beautiful restaurant in Paris. Originally built in 1784, set in the arcades of the Palais-Royal, it has welcomed everyone from Napoléon to Colette to Jean Cocteau—nearly every seat bears a plaque commemorating famous patrons, and you can request to be seated at your idol's table. The mirrored ceiling and Restauration-era glass paintings of goddesses are most beguiling, as so are the dishes of chef Guy Martin. He hails from the mountains of Savoie, so you can find some peasant-luxe dishes among all the foie gras–stuffed ravioli and truffled veal sweetbreads. *17 rue Beaujolais, tel. 01–42–96–56–27. Reservations essential 1 wk in advance. Jacket and tie. AE, DC, MC, V. Closed weekends and Aug. Métro: Palais-Royal.*

$$ **RESTAURANT DU PALAIS-ROYAL.** Tucked away in the northern corner of the magnificent Palais-Royal garden, this pleasant bistro has a lovely terrace and good food. John Dory sautéed with red peppers and onions is among the interesting contemporary dishes. Since this is a wonderful spot for a romantic tête-à-tête, be sure to book in advance, especially during the summer when the terrace tables are hotly sought after. *Jardins du Palais-Royal, 110 Galerie Valois, tel. 01–40–20–00–27. AE, MC, V. Closed Sun. No lunch Sat. Métro: Palais-Royal.*

$–$$ **AUX CRUS DE BOURGOGNE.** This delightfully old-fashioned bistro, with its bright lights and red-check tablecloths, attracts a lively crowd. It opened in 1932 and quickly became popular by serving two luxury items—foie gras and cold lobster with homemade mayonnaise—at surprisingly low prices, a tradition that happily continues. *3 rue Bachaumont, tel. 01–42–33–48–24. V. Closed weekends and Aug. Métro: Sentier.*

$ **L'ARDOISE.** This minuscule storefront, painted white and decorated with enlargements of old sepia postcards of Paris, is the very model of the new contemporary bistros making waves in Paris. Chef Pierre Jay trained at Tour d'Argent, and his creations are first rate: a flan of crab in creamy emulsion of parsley, fresh cod with grilled chips of chorizo sausage, and a *feuillantine au citron*— sugar-glazed, cinammon-sprinkled pastry leaves filled with lemon cream and lemon sections—are all enticing. No wonder L'Ardoise is often crowded. *28 rue du Mont Thabor, tel. 01–42–96–28–18. Reservations essential. MC, V. Closed Mon. Métro: Concorde.*

2ᵉ Arrondissement (La Bourse)

FRENCH

$$ **CHEZ GEORGES.** When you ask sophisticated Parisians—bankers, aristocrats, or antiques dealers—to name their favorite bistro, many choose Georges. The traditional bistro cooking is good—

paris dining

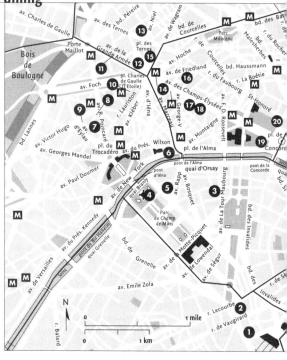

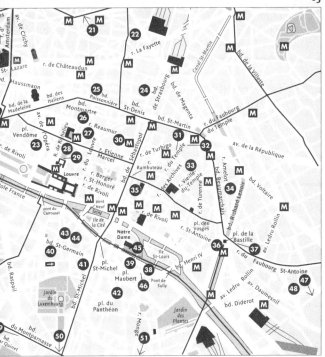

herring, sole, kidneys, steak, and *frites* (fries)—but the atmosphere is better. A wood-paneled entry leads you to an elegant and unpretentious dining room where one long, white-clothed stretch of table lines the mirrored walls. *1 rue du Mail, tel. 01–42–60–07–11. AE, DC, MC, V. Closed Sun. and Aug. Métro: Sentier.*

$$ LE VAUDEVILLE. One of Jean-Paul Bucher's seven Parisian brasseries, Le Vaudeville is filled with well-dressed Parisians (many from the Stock Exchange across the street) and is a good value, thanks to its assortment of prix-fixe menus. Shellfish, house-smoked salmon, and desserts such as profiteroles are particularly fine. Enjoy the handsome 1930s decor and joyful dining until 2 AM daily. *29 rue Vivienne, tel. 01–40–20–04–62. AE, DC, MC, V. Closed Dec. 24. Métro: Bourse.*

3ᵉ Arrondissement (Beaubourg/Marais)

FRENCH

$ LE PAMPHLET. Chef Alain Carrère's modern take on the hearty cooking of the Basque Country and Béarn region of southwestern France has made this Marais bistro popular with an arty local crowd. Beyond the delicious, homey food, what many Parisians love here is that this place feels like a restaurant in the provinces, with its beamed ceiling, homey lamps, generously spaced tables, polite service, and faience that looks like its on loan from *grandmère*. *38 rue Debelleyme, tel. 01–42–72–39–24. MC, V. Closed Sun. No lunch Sat. Métro: St. Sebastien-Froissart.*

NORTH AFRICAN

$ CHEZ OMAR. Popular with a high-voltage fashion crowd—yes, that is Vivienne Westwood having dinner with Alexander McQueen—this is the place to come for couscous, whether you're a die-hard fan or have yet to taste this signature North African dish in all its glory. Proprietor Omar Guerida is famously friendly and speaks English. *47 rue de Bretagne, tel. 01–42–72–36–26. MC, V. No lunch Sun. Métro: Filles du Calvaire.*

4ᵉ Arrondissement (Marais/Ile St-Louis)

FRENCH

$$ ★ **LE GRIZZLI.** It's said that this turn-of-the-century bistro used to have dancing bears out front—thus the name. A real charmer, this is one of the last of the unselfconsciously old-fashioned bistros left in Paris (right down to the creaky spiral staircase leading up to the rest room). The owner gets many of his ingredients—especially the wonderful ham and cheeses—from his native Auvergne. Several dishes are cooked on a hot slate, including the salmon and the lamb. There's an interesting selection of wines from southwest France. 7 rue St-Martin, tel. 01–48–87–77–56. MC, V. Closed Sun. Métro: Châtelet.

$$ **LE VIEUX BISTRO.** Despite the obvious location next to Notre-Dame and the corny name, "the Old Bistro" still pulls a worldly crowd of Parisians, including the likes of Leslie Caron, for home-style Paris comfort food like the sublime slow-simmered *boeuf Bourguignon* (beef stewed in wine). This place really is generations old, and its menu is full of bistro classics, such as beef fillet with marrow, éclairs, and tart Tatin. The decor is nondescript, but the frequently fancy crowd doesn't seem to notice. 14 rue du Cloître-Notre-Dame, tel. 01–43–54–18–95. MC, V. Métro: Hôtel de Ville.

$–$$ **BOFINGER.** One of the oldest, most beautiful, and most popular brasseries in Paris has generally improved since brasserie maestro Jean-Paul Bucher took over. Settle in to one of the tables dressed in crisp white linens, under the gorgeous Art Nouveau glass cupola, and enjoy fine classic brasserie fare, such as oysters, grilled sole, or fillet of lamb. 5–7 rue de la Bastille, tel. 01–42–72–87–82. AE, DC, MC, V. Métro: Bastille.

5ᵉ Arrondissement (Latin Quarter)

FRENCH

$$$$ **LA TOUR D'ARGENT.** On a rooftop famously overlooking Notre-Dame (with prices that are even higher), this temple of *la grande* *cuisine* is not what it used to be—but what is? Still, a meal here can be an event, with its view of Notre-Dame (its nighttime illumination is partly footed by your check and, mind you, many tables are not window-side). The food, though often good, rarely reaches the same heights as this view. But who can resist *caneton Tour d'Argent* (pressed duck), which famously comes with numbered certificate. More nouvelle creations are also featured, along with the best wine cellar in all France. *15 quai de la Tournelle, tel. 01–43–54–23–31. Reservations essential at least 1 wk in advance. Jacket and tie at dinner. AE, DC, MC, V. Closed Mon. Métro: Cardinal Lemoine.*

$$ BISTROT. . . CÔTE MER. A local hit for the professionalism of its staff and its very delicious food, this reasonably priced fish house warms the eye with warm exposed stone walls, marble-top tables, a long brick-color velvet banquette, and old-fashioned tile floors. The dishes warm the stomach, and best bets include a tomato sauté of shrimps with orecchiette pasta and grilled sea bass with black-olive polenta. End it all with crêpes flamed in Grand Marnier—which gives the waiters a chance to ham it up a bit. *16 bd. St-Germain, tel. 01–43–54–59–10. AE, MC, V. Métro: Maubert-Mutualité.*

$$ CHEZ RENÉ. Cozy and appealingly shabby, this reliable address at the eastern end of boulevard St-Germain has satisfied three generations of Parisians, who count on finding dishes from Burgundy, such as *boeuf Bourguignon* (beef stewed in wine) and coq au vin. The dining rooms are cozy, with red-leatherette banquettes and white honeycomb-tile floors. *14 bd. St-Germain, tel. 01–43–54–30–23. MC, V. Closed Sun., Aug., and late Dec.–early Jan. No lunch Sat. Métro: Cardinal Lemoine.*

$ CHANTAIRELLE. Delicious south-central Auvergne cuisine is the specialty here, but the owners of this friendly, good-value spot also want you to fully experience the region, hence the recycled barn timbers, little stone fountain, and oils diffusing scents from the Auvergne. *17 rue Laplace, tel. 01–46–33–18–59. MC, V. Closed Sun. No lunch Sat. Métro: Maubert-Mutualité.*

6e Arrondissement (St-Germain)

FRENCH

$$ ALCAZAR. ★ Englishman Sir Terence Conran's stunning, large new brasserie is one of the chicest and liveliest spots in town. To take in the scene—and quite a scene it is, as this place seats 300 under a skylight roof—opt for a table on the mezzanine, where a long brushed-steel bar gives you a bird's-eye view. Chef Guillaume Lutard has created an appealingly classic menu. *62 rue Mazarine, tel. 01–53–10–19–99. Reservations essential. AE, DC, MC, V. Métro: Odéon.*

$–$$ LE BOUILLON RACINE. Originally a *bouillon*—a Parisian soup restaurant popular at the turn of the century—this two-story place is now a lushly renovated Belle Epoque oasis featuring a good Belgian menu. In honor of Belgium's some 400 brews, it has a wonderful selection of beers. *3 rue Racine, tel. 01–44–32–15–60. Reservations essential. AE, MC, V. Closed Sun. Métro: Odéon.*

$ LA TABLE D'AUDE. Rive Gauche students, senators, and book editors who dine here are on to a good thing, since this jolly restaurant serves some of the best *cuisine regionale* in Paris. Owner Bernard Patou and his wife, Veronique, take a contagious pleasure in serving up the best of their home turf—the Aude, that long narrow region in the Languedoc-Roussillon, which includes Carcassonne, and Castelnaudary, which is famed for its cassoulet. *8 rue de Vaugirard, tel. 01–43–26–36–36. MC, V. Closed Sun. Métro: Odeon.*

SEAFOOD

$$ L'ESPADON BLEU. Chef Jacques Cagna's moderately priced seafood restaurant is a good spot to drop anchor in St-Germain. Yellow walls, blue beams, and mosaic tables with the restaurant's namesake, a blue swordfish, create a stylish nautical feel. The prix-fixe menu is a great deal. *25 rue des Grands Augustins, tel. 01–46–33–00–85. Reservations essential. AE, MC, V. Closed Sun. and Mon. No lunch Sat. Métro: Odéon.*

7ᵉ Arrondissement (Invalides/École Militaire)

FRENCH

\$\$\$\$ JULES VERNE. Top-ranked chef Alain Reix's cuisine—not to mention a location at 400 ft up, on the second level of the Eiffel Tower—make the Jules Verne one of the hardest dinner reservations to get in Paris. Reix's cooking, like the service, has its ups and downs. Come for lunch—a table is easier to snag—and be prepared for the distinctive all-black decor, a rather strange hybrid of *Star Trek* and '70s disco. *Eiffel Tower, tel. 01–45–55–61–44. Reservations essential. Jacket and tie. AE, DC, MC, V. Métro: Bir-Hakeim.*

\$–\$\$ AU BON ACCUEIL. If you want to see what well-heeled Parisians like to eat these days, book a table at this popular bistro as soon as you get to town. The excellent, reasonably priced *cuisine du marché* (daily menu based on what's in the markets) has made it a hit. Be sure to call first, as the owners are planning a major renovation so a temporary closing is in the works. *14 rue de Montessuy, tel. 01–47–05–46–11. Reservations essential. MC, V. Closed Sun. Métro, RER: Pont de l'Alma.*

\$ THOUMIEUX. Delightfully Parisian, this place vibes with red-velour banquettes, yellow walls, and bustling waiters in long, white aprons. Budget prices for decent food like duck confit and cassoulet make this place—owned by the same family for three generations—popular. *79 rue St-Dominique, tel. 01–47–05–49–75. MC, V. Métro: Invalides.*

8ᵉ Arrondissement (Champs-Élysées)

FRENCH

\$\$\$\$ ALAIN DUCASSE. ★ Mega-starred chef Alain Ducasse recently took over the restaurant of the Hotel Plaza-Athénée. You may need to instantly book a Concorde seat to actually catch him at this particular stove—Ducasse now has restaurants around the globe (and never cooks on weekends)—but it will probably be worth it: he's France's top chef. When you taste the *bisque d'homard* (lobster bisque) or the $56 pork belly, you know you are getting the real thing—each is made from as many elements (shell, skin, juice, pan drippings) as possible and offers the absolute quintessence of each dish. Still, for these astronomical prices you might wish for more multi-culti fireworks from the kitchen and a less distant staff. *Hotel Plaza-Athénée, 27 ave. Montaigne, tel. 01–53–67–66–65. Reservations essential weeks in advance. AE, DC, MC, V. Closed Sun. Métro: Alma-Marceau.*

$$$$ LES AMBASSADEURS. ★ Looking as if Madame de Pompadour might stroll in the door any moment, Les Ambassadeurs offers a setting of uniquely ancien régime splendor, with dramatic black-and-white diamond floor, glittering chandeliers, and honey-color marble walls. Chef Dominique Bouchet likes to mix up luxe with more down-to-earth flavors: potato pancakes topped with smoked salmon, caviar-flecked scallops wrapped in bacon with tomato and basil, duck with rutabaga, turbot with cauliflower. It's difficult to fault the distinguished service or the memorable wine list. *10 pl. de la Concorde, tel. 01–44–71–16–16. Reservations essential. Jacket and tie at dinner. AE, DC, MC, V. Métro: Concorde.*

$$$$ LES ÉLYSÉES. ★ Chef Alain Solivères is a passionate cook whose reputation continues to grow in Paris gourmet circles. Come here when you want to treat yourself, since not only is the southern French food of chef Alain Solivères exquisite, but service is also impeccable and the intimate dining room, under a beautiful turn-of-the-century *verrière* (glass ceiling), is the kind of place where you want to linger. Note, though, that it's very busy at midday, so unless you're coming for the good-value lunch menu, dinner is a calmer option. *In Hôtel Vernet, 25 rue Vernet, tel. 01–47–23–43–10. AE, DC, MC, V. Reservations essential. Closed weekends. Métro: George V.*

$$$$ LEDOYEN. Whether you want to eat light or hearty, young chef Christian Le Squer's elegant, beautifully realized menu is a treat. The elegant restaurant tucked away in the quiet gardens flanking the avenue as it runs into the place de la Concorde is a study in the grandiose style of Napoleon III, as revisited by decorator Jacques Grange, with gilded ceilings and walls, plush armchairs, and tables with candelabra. *1 av. Dutuit, on the Carré des Champs-Élysées, tel. 01–47–42–23–23. Reservations essential. AE, DC, MC, V. Closed weekends. Métro: Place de la Concorde, Champs-Élysées–Clemenceau.*

$$$$ PIERRE GAGNAIRE. In a single dish, legendary chef Pierre Gagnaire
★ sensationally brings together unexpected tastes and textures. Two intriguing dishes from a recent menu—it changes seasonally—included duck foie gras wrapped in bacon, and sea bass in herbs with tiny clams. The only negatives are the amateurish service and the brief wine list. *6 rue de Balzac, tel. 01–44–35–18–25. Reservations essential. AE, DC, MC, V. Closed Sun. Métro: Charles-de-Gaulle–Étoile.*

$$$$ TAILLEVENT. Perhaps the most traditional—and this is meant as
★ high praise—of all Paris's luxury restaurants, this grande dame is suddenly the object of a certain uncharacteristic buzz since the arrival of new chef Michel Del Burgo, who has a reputation for food that is at once earthy yet refined. Now he's judiciously revising the menu here, while classics like the *boudin d'homard*—an airy sausage-shape soufflé of lobster—offer continuity with the fabled past. Service is exceptional, the setting—19th-century paneled salons now accented with abstract paintings—is luxe, and the wine list probably one of the top 10 in the world. *15 rue Lamennais, tel. 01–45–63–39–94. Reservations 3–4 wks in advance essential. Jacket and tie. AE, MC, V. Closed weekends and Aug. Métro: Charles-de-Gaulle–Étoile.*

$$ SÉBILLON. The original Sébillon has nurtured chic residents of the fashionable suburb of Neuilly for generations; this elegant, polished branch off the Champs-Élysées continues the tradition. The menu includes lobster salad, lots of shellfish, and—the specialty—roast leg of lamb sliced table-side and served in unlimited quantity. Service is notably friendly. *66 rue Pierre Charron, tel. 01–43–59–28–15. AE, DC, MC, V. Métro: Franklin-D.-Roosevelt.*

CONTEMPORARY

$$ SPOON, FOOD AND WINE. Star chef Alain Ducasse's blueprint of a bistro for the 21st century has been packed ever since it opened in late 1998. What draws the trendy crowd is the playful Asian- and American-inspired menu, the great decor—at night the large white-linen shades on the walls are rolled up to reveal plum upholstery—and that it's so hard to get a reservation. Try the Thai soup, the pasta dishes, and the roast salmon with béarnaise sauce. *14 rue de Marignan, tel. 01–40–76–34–44. Reservations essential. AE, MC, V. Métro: Franklin-D.-Roosevelt.*

9ᵉ Arrondissement (Opéra)

FRENCH

$ CHARTIER. People come to this cavernous turn-of-the-century restaurant more for the bonhomie than the food, which is often rather ordinary. You may find yourself sharing a table as you study the long, old-fashioned menu of such favorites as steak tartare and roast chicken with fries. *7 rue du Faubourg-Montmartre, tel. 01–47–70–86–29. Reservations not accepted. No credit cards. Métro: Rue Montmartre.*

10ᵉ Arrondissement (République/ Gare du Nord)

FRENCH

$$ BRASSERIE FLO. Though it's hard to find—down a passageway near Gare de l'Est—it's worth the effort, for both food and decor. The rich wood and stained glass are typically Alsatian, service is enthusiastic, and brasserie standards such as shellfish and *choucroute* (sauerkraut and sausage) are savory. It's open until 1:30 AM, with a special night-owl menu from 10 PM. *7 cour des Petites Écuries, tel. 01–47–70–13–59. AE, DC, MC, V. Métro: Château d'Eau.*

$–$$ CHEZ MICHEL. Chef Thierry Breton pulls a stylish crowd—despite the drab decor and neighborhood—with his wonderful cuisine du marché and dishes from his native Brittany. Typical of Breton's kitchen are the lasagna stuffed with chèvre and the artichokes and tuna steak with pureed peas. *10 rue Belzunce, tel. 01–44–53–06–20. Reservations essential. MC, V. Closed Sun.–Mon. No lunch Sat. Métro: Gare du Nord.*

11e Arrondissement (Bastille/République)

CHINESE

$$ WOK. Design-it-yourself Oriental stir-fry in a slick, minimalist setting has made this spot a hit with the pennywise hipsters who hang out in the clubs around party-hearty Bastille. You select what type of noodle you want, the waiter brings you a bowl, and then you load up at a buffet with bins of chicken, white fish, shrimp, salmon, beef, vegetables. Mobbed on weekends, this place is fun, nourishing, and cheap. *23 rue des Taillandiers, tel. 01–55–28–88–77. MC, V. Métro: Breguet Sabin, Bastille, or Ledru Rollin.*

FRENCH

$$ LE REPAIRE DE CARTOUCHE. Near the Cirque d'Hiver, in the
★ Bastille, this split-level, '50s-style bistro with dark wood decor is the latest good-value bistro sensation in Paris. Young chef Rodolphe Paquin is a creative and impeccably trained cook who does a stylish take on earthy French regional dishes. The wine list is excellent, with bargains like a Pernand-Vergelesses (red Burgundy) for $20. *99 rue Amelot, tel. 01–47–00–25–86. AE, MC, V. Reservations essential. Closed Sun. No dinner Mon. Métro: Filles du Calvaire.*

12e Arrondissement (Bastille/Gare de Lyon)

FRENCH

$$$ AU TROU GASCON. At this successful Belle Epoque establishment off place Daumesnil, owner Alain Dutournier serves his version of the cuisine of Gascony—a region of outstanding ham, foie gras, lamb, and poultry—and his now-classic white-chocolate mousse. *40 rue Taine, tel. 01–43–44–34–26. AE, DC, MC, V. Closed Sun., Christmas wk, and Aug. No lunch Sat. Métro: Daumesnil.*

$$ LE SQUARE TROUSSEAU. Since fashion designer Jean-Paul Gaultier moved his headquarters nearby, this charming turn-of-the-century bistro has become very chic. You might see a supermodel or two—Claudia Schiffer often comes in when in town—while dining on the homemade foie gras and tender baby chicken with mustard and bread-crumb crust. The house wine is a good value, especially the fruity red Morgon. *1 rue Antoine Vollon, tel. 01–43–44–06–00. MC, V. Métro: Ledru-Rollin.*

13ᵉ Arrondissement (Les Gobelins)

FRENCH

$ LE TERROIR. A jolly crowd of regulars makes this little bistro festive. The solidly classical menu, based on first-rate ingredients from all over France, includes salads with chicken livers or fresh marinated anchovies, calves' liver or monkfish with saffron, and pears marinated in wine. *11 bd. Arago, tel. 01–47–07–36–99. Closed Sun. No lunch Sat. Métro: Les Gobelins.*

14ᵉ Arrondissement (Montparnasse)

FRENCH

$$ CONTRE-ALLÉE. Students and professors crowd this large restaurant, simply decorated with bullfighting posters. The menu has selections such as squid salad with mussels and roast cod with Parmesan; homemade pasta accompanies many dishes. A sidewalk terrace enlivens shady avenue Denfert-Rochereau in summer. The restaurant serves until 11:30 PM. *83 av. Denfert-Rochereau, tel. 01–43–54–99–86. AE, DC, MC, V. No lunch Sat. Métro: Denfert-Rochereau.*

$$ LA COUPOLE. This world-renowned, cavernous place practically defines the term *brasserie*. Many find it too large, too noisy, and too expensive, and no one likes the long wait at the bar before being seated. Still, it has been popular since the days Jean-Paul Sartre and Simone de Beauvoir were regulars, although there are now more bourgeois grandmothers dining here than existential philosophers. *102 bd. du Montparnasse, tel. 01–43–20–14–20. AE, DC, MC, V. Métro: Vavin.*

15ᵉ Arrondissement (Motte-Picquet/Balard)

FRENCH

$$ BISTROT D'HUBERT. In a studied environment that might have sprung from the pages of *Elle Décor*, this popular bistro—frequented by a stylish crowd—serves food that perfectly expresses the countercurrents of the Parisian culinary landscape. The prix-fixe menu is split into two: "tradition" and "innovation." You might have the tuna steak in a "caramel" of balsamic vinegar, or go for the more classic roast lamb. *41 bd. Pasteur, tel. 01–47–34–15–50. Reservations essential. AE, DC, MC, V. Métro: Pasteur.*

$$ PHILIPPE DETOURBE. Amid black lacquer, mirrors, and burgundy-
★ velvet upholstery, sample Detourbe's spectacular contemporary French cooking. The menu changes with every meal and may include smoked salmon filled with cabbage *rémoulade* (cabbage in a creamy dressing) or cod steak with white beans and caramelized endives; desserts are fantastic. The wine list is brief but well chosen; service is friendly and efficient. *8 rue Nicolas Charlet, tel. 01–42–19–08–59. Reservations essential. MC, V. Closed Sun. No lunch Sat. Métro: Pasteur.*

16ᵉ Arrondissement (Arc de Triomphe)

FRENCH

$$–$$$ PRUNIER. Founded in 1925, this seafood restaurant is one of the best—and the prettiest—in Paris. The famous Art Deco mosaics glitter, and the white-marble counters shine with impeccably fresh shellfish. The kitchen not only excels at classic French fish dishes but has added some interesting options, like a *Saintongeaise* plate—raw oysters with grilled sausages. *16 av. Victor-Hugo, tel. 01–44–17–35–85. Reservations essential in upstairs dining room. Jacket and tie. AE, DC, MC, V. Closed Sun.–Mon. Métro: Charles-de-Gaulle–Étoile.*

$$ **LA GRANDE ARMÉE.** Jacques Garcia, France's most talked-about
★ decorator, has unleashed here an exotic Napoléon-III bordello
decor—think black lacquered tables, leopard upholstery, Bordeaux
velvet, plus, of course, a carefully tousled clientele picking at
those dishes that chic Parisians like best these days. *3 av. de la Grande
Armée, tel. 01–45–00–24–77. AE, DC, MC, V. Métro: Charles de Gaulle-
Étoile.*

$$ **LE RELAIS DU PARC.** This bistro-annex is the place to try a lighter
version of Alain Ducasse's cooking for less. Two delicious starters—
the lobster salad, and the baby potatoes with black truffles in a
creamy oxtail-stock sauce—make good meals, followed by cheese
or dessert. Main courses are also excellent, but the desserts could
be better, and wine is overpriced. *55 av. Raymond-Poincaré, tel.
01–44–05–66–10. Reservations essential. AE, DC, MC, V. Métro: Victor
Hugo.*

$ **LE PETIT RÉTRO.** Two types of clientele—men in expensive suits
at noon and well-dressed couples in the evening—frequent this
little bistro with Art Nouveau tiles and bentwood furniture. You
can't go wrong with the daily special written on the chalkboard.
Come when you want a good solid meal, like the perfect *pavé de
boeuf* (thick steak). *5 rue Mesnil, tel. 01–44–05–06–05. MC, V. Closed
Sun. No lunch Mon. Métro: Victor Hugo.*

17ᵉ Arrondissement (Monceau/Clichy/ Arc de Triomphe)

FRENCH

$$$$ **GUY SAVOY.** Top chef Guy Savoy's other five bistros have not
distracted him too much from his handsome luxury restaurant near
the Arc de Triomphe. The oysters in aspic and grilled pigeon
reveal the magnitude of his talent, and the mille-feuille is a
contemporary classic. *18 rue Troyon, tel. 01–43–80–40–61.
Reservations essential. AE, MC, V. Closed Sun. No lunch Sat. Métro:
Charles-de-Gaulle–Étoile.*

ITALIAN

$$ IL BACCELLO. Young chef Raphael Bembaron's talent is pulling crowds to this outpost for first-rate contemporary Italian food. Bembaron trained at Lucas Carton in Paris, Enoteca Pinchiorri in Florence, and at Joia, the gourmet vegetarian restaurant in Milan, and his background comes through in superb dishes like the risotto cooked with Barolo wine and garnished with duck breast and aged Mimolette cheese or langoustines on toothpicks with almond-stuffed green olives on a bed of spelt and broccoli in a pumpkin coulis. This is also a good address for vegetarians. The dining room is done in a sleek (if noisy) minimalist style. *23 rue des Taillandiers, tel. 01–55–28–88–77. MC, V.. Métro: Breguet Sabin, Bastille, or Ledru Rollin.*

NORTH AFRICAN

$$ LE TIMGAD. For a stylish evening out and a night off from French food, try this elegant North African restaurant. Start with a savory *brick* (crispy parchment pastry filled with meat, eggs, or seafood), followed by tasty couscous or succulent *tagine* (meat or poultry that's slowly braised inside a domed pottery casserole). *21 rue de Brunel, tel. 01–45–74–23–70. MC, V. Métro: Argentine.*

18ᵉ Arrondissement (Montmartre)

FRENCH

$ LE MOULIN À VINS. The atmosphere at this popular wine bar/bistro is sepia toned—both it and the surrounding neighborhood evoke old Paris. It's perfect for lunch while touring Montmartre. In the evening it's livelier, when devoted regulars come for the daily short list of hot dishes. *6 rue Burq, tel. 01–45–52–81–27. MC, V. Closed Mon. Métro: Abbesses.*

CAFÉS AND SALONS DE THÉ

Cafés can be found at every bend in Paris; following is a small selection of cafés and *salons de thé* (tearooms) to whet your appetite. **Au Père Tranquille** (16 rue Pierre Lescot, 1ᵉʳ, tel. 01–

45–08–00–34, métro Les Halles) is one of the best places in Paris for people-watching. **Café Beaubourg** (43 rue St-Merri, 4e, tel. 01–48–87–63–96, métro Hôtel-de-Ville), near the Pompidou Center, is a slick, modern spot. **Café Marly** (Cour Napoléon du Louvre, 93 rue de Rivoli, 1er, tel. 01–49–26–06–60, métro Palais-Royal), overlooking the main courtyard of the Louvre, is perfect for an afternoon break or a nightcap and offers a spectacular Belle Epoque decor. **La Crémaillère** (15 pl. du Tertre, 18e, tel. 01–46–06–58–59, métro Anvers) is a veritable monument to fin-de-siècle art in Montmartre. **Ma Bourgogne** (19 pl. des Vosges, 4e, tel. 01–42–78–44–64, métro St-Paul) is a calm oasis for a coffee or a light lunch away from the noisy streets. **Mariage Frères** (30 rue du Bourg-Tibourg, 4e, tel. 01–42–72–28–11, métro Hôtel-de-Ville) is an outstanding tea shop serving 500 kinds of tea, along with delicious tarts. **Salon de Thé du Palais Royal** (Jardins du Palais Royal, 110 Galérie de Valois, 1er, tel. 01–40–20–00–27, métro Palais-Royal) serves tea on a terrace overlooking the gardens of the Palais Royal. **Le Vieux Colombier** (65 rue de Rennes, 7e, tel. 01–45–48–53–81, métro St-Sulpice) is just around the corner from St-Sulpice and the Vieux Colombier Theater.

WINE BARS

Wine bars are a good place to sample a glass (or bottle) of French wine and have an excellent, simple hot meal or just a plate of cheese or charcuterie. Hours can vary widely, so it's best to check ahead; many close around 10 PM. **Aux Bons Crus** (7 rue des Petits-Champs, 1er, tel. 01–42–60–06–45, métro Bourse) is a cramped, narrow venue with an authentically Parisian feel. **Le Baron Rouge** (1 rue Théophile-Roussel, 12e, tel. 01–43–43–14–32, métro Ledru-Rollin) is a noisy and convivial haunt. **Jacques Mélac** (42 rue Léon-Frot, 11e, tel. 01–43–70–59–27, métro Charonne) is named after the jolly owner who bottles several of his own wines—try the chewy red Lirac.

In This Section

Revised and updated by Ian Phillips

shopping

IN THE MOST BEAUTIFUL CITY in the world, it's no surprise to discover that the local greengrocer displays his tomatoes as artistically as Cartier does its rubies. The capital of style, Paris has an endless array of delights to tempt shop-till-you-droppers, from grand couturiers like Dior to the funkiest flea markets. Today every neighborhood seems to reflect a unique attitude and style: Designer extravagance and haute couture characterize avenue Montaigne and rue Faubourg St-Honoré; classic sophistication pervades St-Germain; avant-garde style dresses up the Marais; while a hip feel suffuses the area around Les Halles.

Bargains are surprisingly elusive—it's good to be aware of the slings and arrows of international exchange rates and to know prices at home before you arrive, but if you're hunting for bargains, watch for the word *soldes* (sales): The two main sale seasons are January and July. For nice gifts try the shops in Paris's museums, especially the Louvre, the Musée Carnavalet, the Opéra Garnier, and the Musée des Arts Décoratifs.

If you're from outside the European Union, age 15 and over, and stay in France and/or the European Union for less than six months, you can benefit from Value Added Tax (VAT) reimbursements, known in France as TVA or *détaxe*. To qualify, non-EU residents must spend at least 1,200 francs in a single store on a single day. Refunds vary from 13% to 20.6% and are mailed to you by check or credited to your charge card.

paris shopping

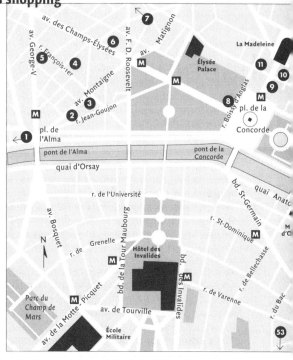

SHOPPING BY NEIGHBORHOOD

Avenue Montaigne

Shopping doesn't come much more chic than on the avenue Montaigne, with its graceful town mansions, which house some of the top names in international fashion: **Chanel, Dior, Nina Ricci, Valentino, Escada, Hanae Mori, Prada, Dolce & Gabbana,** and many more. Neighboring rue François 1er and avenue George V are also lined with many designer boutiques: **Versace, Yves St-Laurent,** and **Balenciaga.**

Champs-Élysées

Cafés and movie theaters keep the once-chic Champs-Élysées active 24 hours a day, but the invasion of exchange banks, car showrooms, and fast-food chains has lowered the tone. Four glitzy 20th-century arcade malls—**Galerie du Lido, Le Rond-Point, Le Claridge,** and **Élysées 26**—capture most of the retail action, not to mention the **Gap** and the **Disney Store.** The opening of a new Peter Marino–designed **Louis Vuitton** boutique and the cosmetic wonder store **Sephora** have reintroduced a touch of elegance.

The Faubourg St-Honoré

This chic shopping and residential street is also quite a political hub. It is home to the Élysée Palace as well as the official residences of the American and British ambassadors. The Paris branches of **Sotheby's** and **Christie's** and renowned antiques galleries such as **Didier Aaron** add artistic flavor. Boutiques include **Hermès, Lanvin, Gucci, Chloé,** and **Christian Lacroix.**

Left Bank

After decades of clustering on the Right Bank's venerable shopping avenues, the high-fashion houses have stormed the Rive Gauche. The first to arrive were **Sonia Rykiel** and **Yves St-**

When it Comes to Getting
Local Currency at an ATM,
Same Thing.

Whether you're in Yosemite or Yemen, using your Visa® card or ATM card with the PLUS symbol is the easiest and most convenient way to get local currency. For example, let's say you're in France. When you make a withdrawal, using your secured PIN, it's dispensed in francs, but is debited from your account in U.S. dollars. This makes it easy to take advantage of favorable exchange rates. And if you need help finding one of Visa's 627,000 ATMs in 127 countries worldwide, visit **visa.com/pd/atm**. We'll make finding an ATM as easy as finding the Eiffel Tower, the Pyramids or even the Grand Canyon.

It's Everywhere You Want To Be.®

SEE THE WORLD
IN FULL COLOR

Fodor's Exploring Guides bring all the great sights vividly to life with hundreds of photographs, fascinating historical background, and colorful anecdotes. Detailed maps and practical information keep you headed in the right direction.

Pair a Fodor's Exploring Guide with your trusted Fodor's Pocket Guide for a complete planning package.

Laurent in the late '60s. Some of the more recent arrivals include **Christian Dior** and **Louis Vuitton.** Rue des St-Pères and rue de Grenelle are lined with designer names.

Louvre–Palais Royal

The elegant and eclectic shops clustered in the 18th-century arcades of the Palais-Royal sell such items as antiques, toy soldiers, cosmetics, jewelry, and vintage designer dresses. The glossy, marble **Carrousel du Louvre** mall, beneath the Louvre Museum, is lighted by an immense inverted glass pyramid. Shops are accompanied by a lively international food court, and all are open on Sunday—still a rare convenience in Paris.

Le Marais

Between the pre-Revolution mansions and tiny kosher food shops that characterize this area are scores of trendy gift and clothing stores, with couturier **Azzedine Alaïa** heading the list of chic boutiques. The Marais is one of the few neighborhoods where shops are open on Sunday.

Opéra to La Madeleine

Three major department stores—**Au Printemps, Galeries Lafayette,** and the British **Marks & Spencer**—dominate boulevard Haussmann, behind Paris's ornate 19th-century Opéra Garnier. Place de la Madeleine is home to two luxurious food stores, **Fauchon** and **Hédiard.**

Place Vendôme and Rue de la Paix

The magnificent 17th-century place Vendôme, home of the Ritz Hotel, and rue de la Paix, leading north from Vendôme, are where you can find the world's most elegant jewelers: **Cartier, Boucheron, Bulgari,** and **Van Cleef and Arpels.** The most exclusive, however, is the discreet **Jar's.**

Rue St-Honoré

A fashionable set makes its way to rue St-Honoré to shop at Paris's most trendy boutique, **Colette**. The street is lined with numerous designer names, while on nearby rue Cambon, you'll find the wonderfully elegant **Maria Luisa** and the main **Chanel** boutique.

DEPARTMENT STORES

Paris's top department stores offer both convenience and style. Most are open Monday through Saturday from 9:30 AM to 7 PM, and some are open until 10 PM one weekday evening.

Au Bon Marché (22 rue de Sèvres, 7ᵉ, tel. 01–44–39–80–00, métro Sèvres-Babylone), the only department store on the Left Bank, is an excellent hunting ground for housewares, men's clothes, and gifts. On the Right Bank, **Bazar de l'Hôtel de Ville** (52–64 rue de Rivoli, 4ᵉ, tel. 01–42–74–90–00, métro Hôtel de Ville), better known as BHV, has minimal fashion offerings but is noteworthy for its enormous basement hardware store. **La Samaritaine** (19 rue de la Monnaie, 1ᵉʳ, tel. 01–40–41–20–20, métro Pont-Neuf or Châtelet) has the Toupary restaurant with magnificent views of the Seine.

The Grand Boulevards are lined with three major department stores: **Au Printemps** (64 bd. Haussmann, 9ᵉ, tel. 01–42–82–50–00, métro Havre-Caumartin, Opéra, or Auber); **Galeries Lafayette** (40 bd. Haussmann, 9ᵉ, tel. 01–42–82–34–56, métro Chaussée d'Antin, Opéra, or Havre-Caumartin); and the British outlet **Marks & Spencer** (35 bd. Haussmann, 9ᵉ, tel. 01–47–42–42–91, métro Havre-Caumartin, Auber, or Opéra).

Budget

Monoprix and **Prisunic** are French dime stores—with scores of branches throughout the city—that stock inexpensive everyday items like toothpaste, groceries, toys, and paper—a little of everything. Both chains carry inexpensive children's clothes and makeup of surprisingly good quality.

MARKETS

The **Marché aux Puces,** on Paris's northern boundary (métro Porte de Clignancourt), which takes place from Saturday through Monday, is a century-old labyrinth of alleyways packed with antiques dealers' booths and junk stalls spreading for more than a square mile; arrive early.

The lively atmosphere that reigns in most of Paris's open-air food markets makes them a sight worth seeing even if you don't want or need to buy anything. Every neighborhood has one, though many are open only a few days each week. Sunday morning till 1 PM is usually a good time to go; Monday the markets are likely to be closed. Many of the better-known markets are in areas you'd visit for sightseeing: **boulevard Raspail** (Between rue de Rennes and rue du Cherche-Midi, 6e, métro Rennes), with a Sunday organic market; **rue de Buci** (6e, métro Odéon), closed Sunday afternoon and Monday; **rue Mouffetard** (5e, métro Monge), best on weekends, near the Jardin des Plantes; **rue Montorgueil** (1er, métro Châtelet–Les Halles), closed Monday; **boulevard Richard Lenoir** (11e, métro Bastille); and **rue Lepic** in Montmartre (18e, métro Blanche or Abbesses), best on weekends.

SHOPPING ARCADES

Paris's 19th-century commercial arcades, called *passages* or *galeries* are the forerunners of the modern mall. Glass roofs, decorative pillars, and mosaic floors give the passages character. The major arcades are on the Right Bank in central Paris. **Galerie Vivienne** (4 rue des Petits-Champs, 2e, métro Bourse) is home to a range of interesting shops, an excellent tearoom, and a quality wine shop.

Passage Jouffroy (12 bd. Montmartre, 2ᵉ, métro Montmartre) is full of shops selling toys, postcards, antique canes, and perfumes. **Passage des Panoramas** (11 bd. Montmartre, 2ᵉ, métro Montmartre), built in 1800, is the oldest of them all. The elegant **Galerie Véro-Dodat** (19 rue Jean-Jacques Rousseau, 1ᵉʳ, métro Louvre) has shops selling old-fashioned toys, contemporary art, and stringed instruments. It is best known, however, for its antiques stores.

SPECIALTY STORES
Accessories, Cosmetics, and Perfumes

Christian Louboutin (19 rue Jean-Jacques Rousseau, 1ᵉʳ, tel. 01–42–36–05–31, métro Louvre) is famous for his wacky but elegant shoes, trademark blood-red soles, and impressive client list (Caroline of Monaco, Catherine Deneuve, Liz Taylor). **Philippe Model** (33 pl. du Marché St-Honoré, 1ᵉʳ, tel. 01–42–96–89–02, métro Tuileries) started off making hats favored by fashionable society ladies and has since added shoes and housewares in two adjacent shops.

Sabbia Rosa (73 rue des Sts-Pères, 6ᵉ, tel. 01–45–48–88–37, métro St-Germain-des-Prés) sells French lingerie favored by celebrities like Catherine Deneuve and Claudia Schiffer. **Sephora** (70 av. de Champs-Elysées, 8ᵉ, tel. 01–53–93–22–50, métro Franklin-D.-Roosevelt; 1 rue Pierre Lescot, in the Forum des Halles, 1ᵉʳ, tel. 01–40–13–72–25, métro Châtelet–Les Halles) is the leading chain of perfume and cosmetics stores in France. Choose from 365 colors of lipstick, browse through the "Cultural Gallery" at the Champs-Élysées store, and even send e-mails for free from the in-store computers.

Bookstores (English-Language)

The scenic open-air bookstalls along the Seine sell secondhand books (mostly in French), prints, and souvenirs. Numerous French-language bookstores—specializing in a wide range of topics, including art, film, literature, and philosophy—are found in the Latin Quarter and around St-Germain-des-Prés. For English-language books try these stores: **Brentano's** (37 av. de l'Opéra, 2ᵉ, tel. 01–42–61–52–50, métro Opéra) is stocked with everything from classics to children's titles. **Galignani** (224 rue de Rivoli, 1ᵉʳ, tel. 01–42–60–76–07, métro Tuileries) is especially known for its extensive range of art and coffee-table books. **Village Voice** (6 rue Princesse, 6ᵉ, tel. 01–46–33–36–47, métro Mabillon) hosts regular literary readings.

Clothing

MENSWEAR

Berluti (26 rue Marbeuf, 8ᵉ, tel. 01–53–93–97–97, métro Franklin-D.-Roosevelt) has been making the most exclusive shoes for men for more than a century. **Charvet** (28 pl. Vendôme, 1ᵉʳ, tel. 01–42–60–30–70, métro Opéra) is the Parisian equivalent of a Savile Row tailor. **Le Printemps de l'Homme** (61 rue Caumartin, 9ᵉ, tel. 01–42–82–50–00, métro Havre-Caumartin) has six floors of designer suits, sportswear, coats, ties, and accessories. **Panoplie** (7 rue d'Argout, 2ᵉ, tel. 01–40–28–90–35, métro Louvre) is one of the best addresses in town for men's designer fashions.

WOMENSWEAR

No matter, say the French, that fewer and fewer of their top couture houses are still headed by compatriots. It's the chic elegance, the classic ambience, the *je ne sais quoi*, that remains undeniably Gallic. Here are some top meccas for Paris chic. **Azzedine Alaïa** (7 rue de Moussy, 4ᵉ, tel. 01–42–72–19–19, métro Hôtel-de-Ville) is the undisputed "king of cling" and the supermodel favorite. **Chanel** (42 av. Montaigne, 8ᵉ, tel. 01–47–23–74–12, métro Franklin-D.-Roosevelt; 31 rue Cambon, 1ᵉʳ, tel. 01–42–86–28–00, métro Tuileries) is helmed by Karl Lagerfeld, a master at updating Coco's signature look with fresh colors and free-spirited silhouettes.

Christian Dior (30 av. Montaigne, 8ᵉ, tel. 01–40–73–54–00, métro Franklin-D.-Roosevelt) installed flamboyant British designer John Galliano as head designer after his triumphant run at Givenchy. **Colette** (213 rue St-Honoré, 1ᵉʳ, tel. 01–55–35–33–90, métro Tuileries) is the most fashionable, most hip, and most hyped store in Paris (and possibly in the world). The ground floor, which stocks design objects, gadgets, and makeup, is generally packed with fashion victims and the simply curious. Upstairs are handpicked fashions, accessories, magazines and books, all of which ooze trendiness.

Sonia Rykiel (175 bd. St-Germain, 6ᵉ, tel. 01–49–54–60–60, métro St-Germain-des-Prés; 70 rue du Faubourg St-Honoré, 8ᵉ, tel. 01–42–65–20–81, métro Concorde) is the queen of French fashion. Since the '60s she has been designing stylish knit separates and has made black her color of predilection.

L'Absinthe (74–76 rue Jean-Jacques Rousseau, 1ᵉʳ, tel. 01–42–33–54–44, métro Les Halles) is a magical address with clothing that's new but looks vintage. **Antik Batik** (18 rue de Turenne, 4ᵉ, tel. 01–48–87–95–95, métro St-Paul) sells hippie-chic, ethnic-inspired clothing, bags, and shoes, which has made the label a hit with in-the-know Parisians and supermodels. **Isabel Marant** (16 rue de Charonne, 11ᵉ, tel. 01–49–29–71–55, métro Ledru-Rollin) is one of the Paris press's favorite designers. French fashionistas flock to her Bastille boutique for her youthful and feminine designs.

Réciproque (88, 89, 92, 95, 101, and 123 rue de la Pompe, 16ᵉ, tel. 01–47–04–30–28, métro Rue de la Pompe) is Paris's largest and most exclusive swap shop; savings on designer wear—Hermès, Dior, Chanel—are significant. **Ventilo** (27 bis, rue du Louvre, 2ᵉ, tel. 01–44–76–83–00, métro Louvre) sells ethnic-inspired fashions to savvy Parisians; On the third floor are housewares and a café serving what is perhaps the best chocolate cake in the world. **Zara** (44 av. des Champs-Élysées,

8e, tel. 01–45–61–52–80, métro Franklin-D.-Roosevelt) is where smart Parisians pick up the latest trends at bargain prices.

Food and Wine

À la Mère de Famille (35 rue du Faubourg-Montmartre, 9e, tel. 01–47–70–83–69, métro Cadet) is well versed in French regional specialties and old-fashioned bonbons, sugar candy, and more. **Les Caves Augé** (116 bd. Haussmann, 8e, tel. 01–45–22–16–97, métro St-Augustin) has been one of the best wine shops in Paris since 1850.

La Maison du Chocolat (56 rue Pierre-Charron, 8e, tel. 01–47–23–38–25, métro Franklin-D.-Roosevelt; 8 bd. de la Madeleine, 9e, tel. 01–47–42–86–52, métro Madeleine; 225 rue du Faubourg–St-Honoré, 8e, tel. 01–42–27–39–44, métro Ternes) is the place for chocolate; take home some or go to the tearoom at rue Pierre Charron or Madeleine.

Housewares and Gifts

Catherine Memmi (32–34 rue St-Sulpice, 6e, tel. 01–44–07–22–28, métro St-Sulpice; 43 rue Madame, 6e, tel. 01–45–48–18–34, métro St-Sulpice) sells wonderfully chic bed linens, bath products, lamps, table settings, furniture, and casual wear—all in elegantly neutral colors.

Christophe Delcourt (76 bis rue Vieille-du-Temple, 3e, tel. 01–42–78–44–97, métro Rambuteau/St-Paul) attracts fashion designers and French film stars, who go mad for his lamps based on old-fashioned drawing tools, pared-down waxed-steel furniture, and sleek wooden tables. **Diptyque** (34 bd. St-Germain, 5e, tel. 01–43–26–45–27, métro Maubert-Mutualité) sells the best scented candles in Paris. **Sentou Galerie** (24 rue du Pont Louis-Philippe, 4e, tel. 01–42–71–00–01, métro St-Paul) has lights created by artists, furniture made by young designers, and funky tableware.

In This Section

Revised and updated by Ian Phillips

outdoor activities and sports

PARISIANS MAY NOT BE AS FANATICAL about exercising as those elsewhere, but in the past few years interest in sports has been growing. A new network of bike paths has seen the number of cyclists boom, there has been a city-wide fad for in-line skating, and the number of gyms has been steadily rising. But the fact remains that most sports facilities tend to be on the outskirts of the city—space for athletic activities at the heart of it tends to be somewhat limited. In fact, it was only in 1997 that laws were passed allowing people to sit, walk, or even play sports on the grass in parks (once strictly forbidden); these days you can enjoy (most) lawns without being reprimanded. One of the best spots for sports in Paris is the Buttes-Chaumont, a park with enough space for soccer and other games. Also good are Paris's two large parks—the Bois de Boulogne, on the western fringe of the city, and the Bois de Vincennes, on the eastern side—where wide-open spaces allow for a variety of activities. (For information on more parks in Paris, see Here and There.)

PARTICIPANT SPORTS
Bicycling

Paris has been making valiant efforts to become more bicycle-friendly. More than 150 km (94 mi) of bicycle lanes now cross the city, notably along rue de Rivoli and boulevard St-Germain. Certain roads are banned to cars altogether on Sunday (including the banks of the Seine along quai de la Tournelle from 9 to 6 mid-March to late fall and the roads alongside the Canal St-Martin from noon to 6 year-round) Paris's two large parks, the Bois de Boulogne (☞ Here and There) and the Bois de Vincennes (métro Porte Dorée, Château de Vincennes) are also good places for biking. Bikes can be rented from the following: **Pariscyclo** (Rond Point de Jardin d'Acclimatation, in the Bois de Boulogne, 16e, tel. 01–47–47–76–50, métro Les Sablons); and **Paris à Vélo, C'est Sympa** (37 bd. Bourdon, 4e, tel. 01–48–87–60–01, métro Bastille); **Paris Vélo Rent a Bike** (2 rue Fer à Moulin, 5e, tel. 01–43–37–59–22, métro Censier-Daubenton).

Health Clubs and Swimming Pools

A number of hotels, gyms, and clubs in the city offer one-day or short-term memberships. **Aquaboulevard de Paris** (4 rue Louis-Armand, 15e, tel. 01–40–60–10–00, métro Balard) has a gym, Turkish baths, and the city's best swimming pool, complete with giant slide and wave machine (150 francs per day). **Club Quartier Latin** (19 rue de Pontoise, 5e, tel. 01–55–42–77–88, métro Maubert Mutualité) has a 30-meter skylighted pool, a climbing wall, squash courts, and exercise equipment (85 francs per day and 75 francs per 40 minutes of squash). **Espace Vit'Halles** (48 rue Rambuteau, 3e, tel. 01–42–77–21–71, métro Rambuteau) has a broad range of aerobics classes (100 francs a class), exercise machines, a sauna, and a steam bath.

Pilates Studio (39 rue du Temple, 4e, tel. 01–42–72–91–74, métro Hôtel de Ville) may just be based in a three-room apartment, but it attracts numerous celebrities, such as actress. Kristin Scott Thomas and French *Vogue* editor Joan Juliet Buck. A one-hour private class costs 310 francs; classes for two are 210 francs per person. The **Piscine des Halles** (Entrance on pl. de la

Rotonde, in Forum des Halles, 1er, tel. 01–42–36–98–44) is a 50-meter public pool; admission is 25 francs; call for hours. The **Ritz Health Club** (Hotel Ritz, pl. Vendôme, 1er, tel. 01–43–16–30–60, métro Opéra), as fancy as the hotel, has a swimming pool, sauna, steam room, Jacuzzi, exercise machines, and aerobics classes (all for 600 francs on weekdays, 700 francs on weekends). **Sofitel Paris Vitatop Club** (8 rue Louis-Armand, 15e, tel. 01–45–54–79–00, métro Balard) has a 15-meter pool, a sauna, a steam room, and a Jacuzzi, plus a stunning view of the Paris skyline (200 francs per day and free to hotel guests).

Rollerblading

A popular site for rollerblading is along the promenade Plantée, running along the former viaduct in the 12e arrondissement, as well as along the Seine and the Canal St-Martin (☞ Bicycling, *above*). Every Friday night starting at 10, thousands of advanced skaters gather at place de l'Italie to rollerblade together through Paris (roads are blocked off); for details check the Web site (www.pari-roller.com). A more leisurely three-hour route is organized on Sunday at 2:30 PM and leaves from Roller Locations Nomades near the place de la Bastille. Rollerblades can be rented from **Bike'n'Roller** (6 rue St-Julien le Pauvre, 5^e, tel. 01–44–07–35–89) for 30 francs for three hours and 60 francs per day. **Roller Location Nomades** (37 bd. Bourdon, 4^e, tel. 01–44–54–07–44) rents skates for 50–60 francs per day.

SPECTATOR SPORTS

Information on upcoming events can be found in the weekly guide **Pariscope,** on posters around the city, or by calling the ticket agencies of **FNAC** (tel. 08–03–80–88–03) or the **Virgin Megastore** (tel. 08–03–02–30–24). A wide range of sporting events takes place at the **Palais Omnisports de Paris-Bercy** (8 bd. de Bercy, 12e, tel. 08–03–03–00–31, métro Bercy). Details of events are also on their Web site: www.bercy.com The **Parc des**

Princes (24 rue du Cdt. Guilbaud, 16ᵉ, tel. 01–42–88–02–76, métro Porte d'Auteuil) is where the city's soccer team, Paris St-Germain, plays its home matches.

Roland-Garros (2 av. Gordon Bennett, 16ᵉ, tel. 01–47–43–48–00, métro Porte d'Auteuil) is the venue for the French Open tennis tournament in May. **Stade de France** (St-Denis, tel. 01–55–93–00–00, RER La Plaine–Stade de France) was built for the World Cup in 1998 and is now home to the French national soccer and rugby teams.

Pick a Park

- **BASSIN DE L'ARSENAL.** This small canal-side park, complete with a café-restaurant, is a peaceful spot to eat lunch and watch the boats. Napoléon created the canal to increase water movement through the city, and Jacques Chirac commissioned the park in the 1980s. Métro: Bastille.

- **PARK ANDRÉ-CITROËN.** Named for the automobile magnate, this park has greenhouses, playful fountains, shallow waterways, carpetlike lawns you can play on, and trees arranged like an army regiment. Métro: Balard.

- **PARC DE BERCY.** Constructed on the riverside site of the city's 19th-century wine warehouses, across the Seine from the giant National Library, this designer park has flower beds, arbors, lawns, lily ponds, a rose garden, and symbolically, a small vineyard. Cobblestone alleys lined with centurion trees also pay homage to the site's past. Métro: Bercy or Cours St-Émilion.

- **PARC GEORGES-BRASSENS.** Once an abattoir (slaughterhouse), this park has secluded paths, rocks to climb, Ping-Pong, and a theater. There's also a huge used-book market on weekends. Métro: Porte de Vanves.

- **PARC MONCEAU.** In the posh 8ᵉ arrondissement, this garden was the setting for steamy love scenes in Zola's La Curée. Besides au pairs pushing strollers you'll find fake grottoes, made-to-look-ancient Greek sculptures, a waterfall, a pyramid, and the Musée Cernuschi—a small museum of Chinese art. Métro: Monceau.

- **SQUARE DU VERT-GALANT.** Created in 1884, this square on the tip of the Ile de la Cité is the place to go to smooch, catch a sunset, and watch the Seine flow by. Métro: Pont-Neuf.

In This Section

Revised and updated by Alexander Lobrano

nightlife and the arts

WITH A HERITAGE THAT INCLUDES the cancan, the Folies-Bergère, the Moulin Rouge, Mistinguett, and Josephine Baker, Paris is one city where no one has ever had to ask, "Is there any place exciting to go to tonight?" Today the city's nightlife and arts scenes are still filled with pleasures. Hear a chansonnier belt out Piaf, take in a Victor/Victoria show, catch a Molière play at the Comédie Française, or perhaps spot Madonna at the Buddha Bar. Information about what's going on in the city can be found in the weekly magazines (published every Wednesday) *Pariscope* (which has an English section), *L'Officiel des Spectacles*, and *Figaroscope* (a supplement to Le Figaro newspaper). The **Paris Tourist Office** (☞ Visitor Information in Practical Information) has a 24-hour hot line in English (tel. 08–36–68–31–12) and a Web site (www.paris-touristoffice.com) listing events.

The best place to buy tickets is at the venue itself; try to purchase in advance, as many of the more popular performances sell out. Also try your hotel or a travel agency, such as **Paris-Vision** (1 rue Auber, 9ᵉ, tel. 01–40–06–01–00, métro Opéra). Tickets for most concerts can be bought at **FNAC** (especially 1–5 rue Pierre Lescot, Forum des Halles, 3rd level down, 1ᵉʳ, tel. 01–49–87–50–50, métro Châtelet–Les Halles).

The **Virgin Megastore** (52 av. des Champs-Élysées, 8ᵉ, tel. 08–03–02–30–24, métro Franklin-D.-Roosevelt) also sells theater and concert tickets. Half-price tickets for many same-day theater performances are available at the **Kiosques Théâtre** (Across from 15 pl. de la Madeleine, métro Madeleine and

Montparnasse-Bienvenüe; and Outside Gare Montparnasse on pl. Raoul Dautry, 15e, métro Madeleine métro Montparnasse-Bienvenüe); both are open Tuesday–Saturday 12:30–8 and Sunday 12:30–4. Expect to pay a 16-franc commission per ticket and to wait in line.

NIGHTLIFE

The City of Light truly lights up after dark. So, if you want to paint the town *rouge* after dutifully pounding the parquet in museums all day, there's a dazzling array of options to discover. The hottest spots are around Ménilmontant, the Bastille, and the Marais. The Left Bank is definitely a lot less happening. The Champs-Élysées is making a comeback, though the clientele remains predominantly foreign. Take note: The last métro runs between 12:30 AM and 1 AM (you can take a taxi, but they can be hard to find, especially on weekend nights).

Bars and Clubs

It helps to be famous—or look like a model—to get into **Les Bains** (7 rue du Bourg-l'Abbé, 3e, tel. 01–48–87–01–80, métro Étienne-Marcel), a forever-trendy club (closed Monday). **Barrio Latino** (46/48 rue du Faubourg St-Antoine, 11e tel. 01–55–78–84–75, métro Bastille) is the latest addition to the Bastille party district, with a decor that is a lush cross of Casbah, old Havana, and SoHo Loft.

Batofar (11 quai François Mauriac, 11e, 01–56–29–10–00, métro Bibliothèque) is an old lighthouse tug, now refitted to include a bar, a club, and a concert venue that's become one of the hippest spots in town. **Buddha Bar** (8 rue Boissy d'Anglas, 8e, tel. 01–53–05–90–00, métro Concorde) offers a knockout setting, with its towering gold-painted Buddha contemplating enough Dragon Empress screens and colorful chinoiserie for five MGM movies. When it opened several years ago, Madonna used to make this scene, along with a lot of other glitterati.

Le Cabaret (68 rue de Charonne, 8ᵉ, tel. 01–42–89–44–14, métro Franklin-D.-Roosevelt) used to be just that; now there are still cabaret acts, as well as dancing to soul and funk. **Café Charbon** (109 rue Oberkampf, 11ᵉ, tel. 01–43–57–55–13, métro St-Maur, Parmentier) is a beautifully restored 19th-century café with a trendsetting crowd. **Le Comptoir** (5 rue Monsieur-Le-Prince, 6ᵉ, tel. 01–43–29–12–05, métro Odéon) is a traditional wine bar serving Burgundy and Bordeaux by the glass. **L'Élysée Montmartre** (72 bd. de Rochechouart, 18ᵉ, tel. 01–44–92–45–45, métro Anvers) hosts the hottest club nights in Paris on Saturday (during the week it's a concert hall).

Finnegan's Wake (9 rue des Boulangers, 5ᵉ, tel. 01–46–34–23–65, métro Jussieu) attracts a mixed Franco-British clientele with its Guinness on tap and Irish music. If you ever get homesick to hear English, Paris has quite a few other pubs, including the Auld Alliance, Connolly's Corner, and the Cricketeer. **Le Fumoir** (6 rue Amiral de Coligny, 1ᵉʳ, tel. 01–42–92–00–24, métro Louvre), a fashionable spot for cocktails, has a large bar, library, and comfy leather couches.

Man Ray (34 rue Marbeuf, 8ᵉ, tel. 01–56–88–36–36, métro Franklin-D.-Roosevelt), owned by Sean Penn, Johnny Depp, and Mick Hucknall, has a spacious mezzanine bar overlooking an Asian-inspired dining room. **Le What's Up Bar** (15 rue Daval, 11ᵉ, tel. 01–48–05–88–33, métro Bastille) is a hip, modern spot where trendy DJs play house and garage music after 10:30 PM; on weekends there's a 50-franc cover.

GAY AND LESBIAN BARS AND CLUBS

Gay and lesbian bars and clubs are mostly concentrated in the Marais and include some of the most happening addresses in the city. **Le Dépôt** (10 rue aux Ours, 3ᵉ, tel. 01–44–54–96–96, métro Etienne Marcel) is a bar, club, and back room for men. The mostly male crowd at **L'Open Café** (17 rue des Archives, 4ᵉ, tel. 01–42–72–26–18, métro Hôtel-de-Ville) comes for the sunny decor and convivial ambience.

Le Pulp! (25 bd. Poissonnière, 2ᵉ, tel. 01–40–26–01–93, métro Grands Boulevards) is one of the few lesbian-only nightclubs in Paris. **Queen** (102 av. des Champs-Élysées, 8ᵉ, tel. 01–53–89–08–90, métro George-V) is one of the hottest nightspots in Paris: Although it's predominantly gay, everyone else lines up to get in, too.

HOTEL BARS

Paris's hotel bars are highly popular nostalgic spots as well as quiet, elegant places to talk. **Bristol** (112 rue du Faubourg–St-Honoré, 8ᵉ, tel. 01–53–43–43–42, métro Miromesnil). **Lutétia** (45 bd. Raspail, 6ᵉ, tel. 01–49–54–46–09, métro Sèvres-Babylone). **Ritz Hemingway Bar** (15 pl. Vendôme, 1ᵉʳ, tel. 01–43–16–33–65, métro Opéra).

Cabaret

Paris's cabarets are household names, though mostly tourists go to them these days. Prices range from 200 francs (simple admission plus one drink) to more than 800 francs (dinner plus show). **Crazy Horse** (12 av. George-V, 8ᵉ, tel. 01–47–23–32–32, métro Alma-Marceau) is one of the best-known cabarets, with pretty dancers and raunchy routines.

Au Lapin Agile (22 rue des Saules, 18ᵉ, tel. 01–46–06–85–87, métro Lamarck-Caulaincourt), in Montmartre, considers itself the doyen of cabarets and is a miraculous survivor from the early 20th century. You'll find no froufrou here, just a chunk of Montmartre history. Picasso immortalized the place in a painting that was sold for $48 million and now is in New York's Metropolitan Museum. Prices here are lower than elsewhere, but then it is more a large bar than a full-blown cabaret.

Lido (116 bis av. des Champs-Élysées, 8ᵉ, tel. 01–40–76–56–10, métro George-V) stars the famous Bluebell Girls; the owners claim that no show in Las Vegas can rival it for special effects. That old favorite at the foot of Montmartre, **Moulin Rouge** (Pl.

Blanche, 18e, tel. 01–53–09–82–82, métro Blanche), mingles the Doriss Girls, the cancan, and a horse in an extravagant spectacle. **Paradis Latin** (28 rue du Cardinal Lemoine, 5e, tel. 01–43–25–28–28, métro Cardinal Lemoine) is the liveliest and trendiest cabaret on the Left Bank.

Jazz Clubs

For nightly schedules consult the specialty magazines *Jazz Hot* or *Jazz Magazine*. Nothing gets going till 10 PM or 11 PM; entry prices vary widely from about 40 francs to more than 100 francs. At the Méridien Hotel, near Porte Maillot, the **Lionel Hampton Jazz Club** (81 bd. Gouvion-St-Cyr, 17e, tel. 01–40–68–30–42, métro Porte Maillot) hosts a roster of international jazz players.

New Morning (7 rue des Petites-Écuries, 10e, tel. 01–45–23–51–41, métro Château-d'Eau) is a premier spot for serious fans of avant-garde jazz, as well as folk and world music. The greatest names in French and international jazz have been playing at **Le Petit Journal** (71 bd. St-Michel, 5e, tel. 01–43–26–28–59, RER Luxembourg) for decades; it now specializes in Dixieland jazz (it's closed Sunday).

Rock, Pop, and World Music Venues

Upcoming concerts are posted on boards in FNAC and Virgin Megastores. **Le Bataclan** (50 bd. Voltaire, 11e, tel. 01–48–06–28–12, métro Oberkampf) is an intimate venue for live rock, rap, and reggae. **L'Élysée Montmartre** (☞ Bars and Clubs, *above*) is one of the prime venues for emerging French and international rock groups.

L'Olympia (28 bd. des Capucines, 9e, tel. 01–47–42–25–49, métro Madeleine), a legendary venue once favored by Jacques Brel and Edith Piaf, still plays host to leading French vocalists. **Zenith** (Parc de la Villette, 19e, tel. 01–42–08–60–00, métro Porte-de-Pantin) stages large rock shows.

THE ARTS
Classical Music

Classical- and world-music concerts are held at the **Cité de la Musique** (221 av. Jean-Jaurès, 19ᵉ, tel. 01–44–84–44–84, métro Porte de Pantin). The **Salle Pleyel** (252 rue du Faubourg–St-Honoré, 8ᵉ, tel. 01–45–61–53–00, métro Ternes) is Paris's principal home of classical music.

The **Théâtre des Champs-Élysées** (15 av. Montaigne, 8ᵉ, tel. 01–49–52–50–50, métro Alma-Marceau), an Art Deco temple, hosts concerts and ballet. Paris has a never-ending stream of inexpensive lunchtime and evening concerts in churches, some scheduled as part of the **Festival d'Art Sacré** (tel. 01–44–70–64–10 for information) between mid-November and Christmas. **Churches** with classical concerts (often free) include (☞ Here and There for addresses): **Notre-Dame, Sainte-Chapelle, St-Eustache, St-Germain-des-Prés, St-Julien-Le-Pauvre, St-Louis-en-l'Ile,** and **St-Roch.**

Dance

The **Opéra Garnier** (Pl. de l'Opéra, 9ᵉ, tel. 08–36–69–78–68, www.opera-de-paris.fr, métro Opéra) is home to the reputable Paris Ballet. The **Opéra de la Bastille** (Pl. de la Bastille, 12ᵉ, tel. 08–36–69–78–68, www.opera-de-paris.fr, métro Bastille) occasionally hosts major dance troupes, often modern and avant-garde in tenor. Both here and at the Opéra Garnier venue, ballet production ticket prices usually range from about 45 to 270 francs.

At the **Théâtre de la Bastille** (76 rue de la Roquette, 11ᵉ, tel. 01–43–57–42–14, métro Bastille), innovative modern dance companies perform. The **Théâtre de la Ville** (2 pl. du Châtelet, 4ᵉ, tel. 01–42–74–22–77 for both, métro Châtelet; 31 rue des Abbesses, 18ᵉ, métro Abbesses) is Paris's temple of contemporary dance.

Film

Parisians are far more addicted to the cinema as an art form than even Londoners or New Yorkers, as revealed by the number of movie theaters in the city. Many theaters, especially in principal tourist areas such as the Champs-Élysées, St-Germain-des-Prés, Les Halles, and the boulevard des Italiens near the Opéra, show first-run films in English. Check the weekly guides for a movie of your choice. Look for the initials *v.o.*, which mean *version originale*, that is, not dubbed. Cinema admission runs from 37 to 51 francs; many theaters reduce rates slightly on Monday and for some morning shows. Most theaters will post two show times: The first is the *séance*, when commercials, previews, and sometimes short films start, and the second is the actual feature presentation time, which is usually 10–20 minutes later. Paris has many small cinemas showing classic and independent films, especially in the Latin Quarter. Screenings are often organized around retrospectives (check "Festivals" in weekly guides).

One of the best venues for classic French and international films (Wednesday–Saturday) is the **Cinémathèque Française** (42 bd. de Bonne-Nouvelle, tel. 01–47–04–24–24, métro Bonne-Nouvelle and Palais de Chaillot, 7 av. Albert de Mun, tel. 01–55–73–16–80, métro Trocadéro). The **Max Linder Panorama** (24 bd. Poissonnière, 9e, tel. 01–48–24–88–88, métro Rue Montmartre) frequently shows classics on its big screen.

Opera

Getting tickets to the opera can be difficult on short notice, so it's a good idea to plan ahead. For the season's schedule, contact the **Opéra de la Bastille** (120 rue de Lyon, Paris 75012) in advance. Bookings by mail begin roughly two months before the date of performance. Buying from scalpers is not recommended, as they have been known to sell counterfeit tickets.

The **Opéra de la Bastille** (Pl. de la Bastille, 12e, tel. 08–36–69–78–68, www.opera-de-paris.fr, métro Bastille), a modern auditorium, has taken over the role as Paris's main opera house from the Opéra Garnier (☞ Dance, *above*). However, nothing beats seeing a grand production of a Verdi or Mozart opera within the splendor of Opéra Garnier, and the good news is that this historic house still hosts a limited number of Opéra National de Paris productions every season. Note that if a *Don Giovanni* is presented, it is only mounted for a minirun of one to two weeks, not in a repertory schedule throughout the season. At both the Bastille and Garnier houses, opera price tickets range from about 70 to 625 francs; cheaper seats in the Garnier house are sometimes view-obstructed.

The **Opéra Comique** (5 rue Favart, 2ᵉ, tel. 01–42–44–45–46, métro Richelieu-Drouot) is a lofty old hall where comic operas are often performed. Better known as the Théâtre du Châtelet, the **Théâtre Musical de Paris** (Pl. du Châtelet, 1ᵉʳ, tel. 01–40–28–28–40, métro Châtelet) has built up a strong reputation for opera and other productions.

Theater

A number of theaters line the Grand Boulevards between Opéra and République, but there is no Paris equivalent to Broadway or the West End. Shows are mostly in French. **Bouffes du Nord** (37 bis bd. de la Chapelle, 10ᵉ, tel. 01–46–07–34–50, métro La Chapelle) is the wonderfully atmospheric theater that is home to English director Peter Brook.

The **Comédie-Française** (Pl. André-Malraux, 1ᵉʳ, tel. 01–44–58–15–15, métro Palais-Royal) is a distinguished venue that stages classical French drama. The **Théâtre de la Huchette** (23 rue de la Huchette, 5ᵉ, tel. 01–43–26–38–99, métro St-Michel), a tiny Left Bank theater, has been staging Ionesco's *The Bald Soprano* every night since 1950. **Théâtre de l'Odéon** (Pl. de l'Odéon, 6ᵉ, tel. 01–44–41–36–36, métro Odéon) has made pan-European theater its primary focus.

Fruity Brewski?

Tired of plain-old French wine? For a change, try some of these other flavorful beverages while toasting the town:

- **BECASSE:** a Belgian strawberry-flavored beer.
- **CALVADOS:** an apple brandy.
- **CIDRE:** cider; choose between doux (sweet) and sec (dry).
- **DIABOLO:** tonic water flavored with grenadine.
- **KIR:** white wine flavored with cassis.
- **KRIEK:** black cherry–flavored beer.
- **MONACO:** a light beer with grenadine syrup.
- **PANACHÉ:** a mixture of half beer and half lemonade.
- **PÊCHERESSE:** peach-flavored beer.
- **PELFORTH FRAMBOISE:** dark beer with raspberry flavoring.

In This Section

Revised and updated by Christopher Mooney

where to stay

WINDING STAIRCASES, FLOWER-FILLED WINDOW BOXES, concierges who seem to have stepped from a 19th-century novel—all of these still exist in Paris hotels. So do grand rooms with marble baths, Belle Epoque lobbies, and polished staff at your beck and call. In Paris there are wonderful hotels for every taste and budget.

Our criteria when selecting the hotels reviewed below were quality, location, and character. Fewer hotels are listed in outlying arrondissements (the 10^e to the 20^e) because these are farther from the major sights. Generally, there are more hotels on the Right Bank offering luxury—or at any rate formality—than there are on the Left Bank, where hotels are frequently smaller and richer in old-fashioned ambience. In Paris's oldest quarters hotel rooms are generally much smaller than their American counterparts. Although air-conditioning has become de rigueur in middle- to higher-price hotels, it is generally not a prerequisite for comfort (Paris's hot weather season doesn't usually last long).

Despite the huge choice of hotels, you should always reserve well in advance, especially if you're determined to stay in a specific place. You can do this by telephoning or faxing ahead, then asking for written or faxed confirmation of your reservation, detailing the duration of your stay, the price, the location and type of your room (single or double, twin beds or double), and the bathroom (shower—*douche*—or bath—*baignoire*—private or shared).

Almost all Paris hotels charge extra for breakfast, with prices ranging from 30 francs to more than 200 francs per person in luxury establishments. For anything more than the standard Continental breakfast of café au lait and croissants, the price will be higher. You may be better off finding the nearest café. A nominal *séjour* (lodging) tax of 7 francs per person, per night is charged to pay for promotion of tourism in Paris.

CATEGORY	COST*
$$$$	over 1,750 frs
$$$	1,000 frs–1,750 frs
$$	600 frs–1,000 frs
$	under 600 frs

All prices are for a standard double room, including 20.6% tax and service.

1ᵉʳ Arrondissement (Louvre/Les Halles)

$$$$ Costes. ★ Jean-Louis and Gilbert Costes's sumptuous hotel is the darling of the fashion and media set. Conjuring up the palaces of Napoléon III, salons are swathed in rich garnet and bronze tones and contain a luxurious mélange of patterned fabrics, heavy swags, and enough brocade and fringe to blanket the Champs-Élysées. The seductive, go-for-baroque bar, with its labyrinth of little rooms and secluded nooks, is *the* place in Paris to be seen trying not to be seen. Thanks to decorating genius Jacques Garcia, this hotel is the tops for taste in Paris. *239 rue St-Honoré, 75001, tel. 01–42–44–50–50, fax 01–42–44–50–01,. 85 rooms. Restaurant, bar, air-conditioning, in-room data ports, in-room safes, room service, indoor pool, sauna, exercise room, laundry service. AE, DC, MC, V. Métro: Tuileries. www.hotelcostes.com*

$$$$ Meurice. ★ One of the finest hotels in the world has become even finer—thanks to the millions of the sultan of Brunei, the fabled restaurant and the elaborately gilded 18th-century Rococo salons have been entirely restored, and the rooms—adorned with Persian carpets, marble mantelpieces, and ormolu clocks—are now more opulent and soigné than ever, if that's possible (book well in advance for a room or a suite overlooking the Tuileries Gardens). The hotel's restaurant is set in one of the most lavishly opulent rooms in the city. *228 rue de Rivoli, 75001, tel. 01–44–58–10–10, fax 01–44–58–10–15. 160 rooms, 36 suites. 2 Restaurants, bar, air-conditioning, in-room data ports, in-room safes, minibars, concierge, sauna, no-smoking rooms, room service, laundry service, business services. AE, DC, MC, V. Métro: Tuileries, Concorde. www.meuricehotel.com*

$$$$ Régina. In the handsome place des Pyramides, this 100-year-old Art Nouveau gem oozes old-fashioned grandeur in both public spaces and guest rooms. There are a sublime Belle Epoque lounge and fine antiques throughout. Request a room on rue de Rivoli facing the Louvre and the Tuileries Gardens. *2 rue des Pyramides, 75001, tel. 01–42–60–31–10, fax 01–40–15–95–16. 129 rooms, 15 suites. Restaurant, bar, air-conditioning, in-room safes, no-smoking rooms, room service, laundry service, meeting rooms. AE, DC, MC, V. Métro: Tuileries. www.regina-hotel.com*

$$$$ Ritz. Founded as a temple of luxury by César Ritz, this legendary place has been regilded at a cost of $150 million by owner Mohammed al-Fayed (whose son Dodi, with Diana, Princess of Wales, set out on their fatal car ride after dining here in August 1997). Of course, there are really two Ritzes. The first is the gilded place Vendôme wing—this is where Gary Cooper serenaded Audrey Hepburn in *Love in the Afternoon* and features the legendary suites named after former residents, such as Marcel Proust and Coco Chanel. The newer wing, off the back of the building, remains surprisingly (disappointingly?) intimate. Don't miss the famous Hemingway Bar (which the writer claimed to have "liberated" in 1944). *15 pl. Vendôme, 75001, tel. 01–43–16–30–30,*

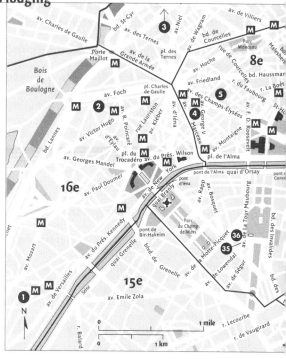

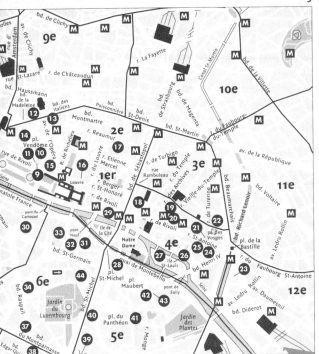

fax 01–43–16–36–68. 142 *rooms, 45 suites. 3 restaurants, 2 bars, air-conditioning, in-room safes, room service, indoor pool, beauty salon, health club, shops, laundry service, meeting rooms, parking (fee). AE, DC, MC, V. Métro: Opéra.* www.parisritz.com

$$$–$$$$ ★ **Vendôme.** This hotel has the best guest-to-staff ratio in Paris and every luxury perk imaginable. Rooms are in sumptuous, Second Empire style and bathrooms are over the top. Best of all, besides a videophone for checking out visitors at the door, is the fully automated bedside console that controls the lights, curtains, and electronic do-not-disturb sign. *1 pl. Vendôme, 75001, tel. 01–42–60–32–84, fax 01–49–27–97–89. 19 rooms, 10 suites. Restaurant, bar, air-conditioning, room service, in-room safes, in-room modem lines, laundry service. AE, DC, MC, V. Métro: Concorde, Opéra.*

$$ **Britannique.** Open since 1870, the Britannique blends courteous English service with old-fashioned French elegance. It has retained its handsome winding staircase and has well-appointed, soundproof rooms in chic, warm tones. *20 av. Victoria, 75001, tel. 01–42–33–74–59, fax 01–42–33–82–65. 40 rooms. Bar, in-room safes. AE, DC, MC, V. Métro: Châtelet.*

$ ★ **Louvre Forum.** This hotel is a find: Smack in the center of town, it has a friendly feel and clean, comfortable, well-equipped rooms (minibars, satellite TV). *25 rue du Bouloi, 75001, tel. 01–42–36–54–19, fax 01–42–33–66–31. 27 rooms. Bar, minibars. AE, DC, MC, V. Métro: Louvre.*

2ᵉ Arrondissement (La Bourse)

$$ **Grand Hôtel de Besançon.** This terrific hotel, with its very Parisian cream-color facade and wrought-iron balconies, has it all—intimacy, comfort, affordability, and a location on a delightful, pedestrian market street near Les Halles, the Pompidou Center, and the Marais. Rooms are classically decorated with French upholsteries and period reproductions, and despite the busy area nearby, they are quiet. *56 rue Montorgueil, 75002, tel. 01–42–*

36–41–08, fax 01–45–08–08–79. 11 rooms, 14 suites. In-room modem lines, in-room safes, laundry service AE, DC, MC, V. Métro: Etienne-Marcel, Les Halles.

$$ **Hôtel de Noailles.** With a nod to the work of postmodern designers like Putman and Starck, this new-wave inn (part of the Tulip Inn group) is a star among Paris's new crop of well-priced, style-driven boutique hotels. Though not to everyone's taste, rooms are imaginatively decorated with funky furnishings and contemporary details. *9 rue de Michodière, 75002, tel. 01–47–42–92–90, fax 01–49–24–92–71. 58 rooms. Bar, air-conditioning, laundry service. AE, DC, MC, V. Métro: Opéra.*

3ᵉ Arrondissement (Beaubourg/Marais)

$$$$ **Pavillon de la Reine.** On lovely place des Vosges, this magnificent mansion, reconstructed from original plans, is filled with Louis XIII–style fireplaces and antiques. Ask for a duplex with French windows overlooking the first of two flower-filled courtyards behind the historic Queen's Pavilion. Breakfast is served in the vaulted cellar, *digestifs* in front of the salon's gargantuan fireplace. *28 pl. des Vosges, 75003, tel. 01–40–29–19–19; 800/447–7462 in the U.S., fax 01–40–29–19–20. 30 rooms, 25 suites. Bar, breakfast room, air-conditioning, room service, laundry service, parking (free). AE, DC, MC, V. Métro: Bastille, St-Paul.*

4ᵉ Arrondissement (Marais/Ile St-Louis)

$$$ **Hôtel du Jeu de Paume.** The showpiece of this lovely 17th-century hotel on the Ile St-Louis is the stone-walled, vaulted lobby–cum–breakfast room. It stands on an erstwhile court where French aristocrats once played *jeu de paume*, an early version of tennis using palm fronds. The bright rooms are nicely done up in butter yellow, with rustic antiques, tasteful objets and bric-a-brac, beamed ceilings, and damask upholsteries. The little garden is a haven of sun-drenched tranquillity. *54 rue St-Louis-en-l'Ile, 75004, tel. 01–43–26–14–18, fax 01–40–46–02–76. 30 rooms, 1 junior suite. Bar, baby-*

sitting, laundry service, sauna, health club, meeting rooms. AE, DC, MC, V. Métro: Pont-Marie. www.jeudepaumehotel.com

\$\$ Axial Beaubourg. A solid bet in the Marais, this hotel in a 16th-century building has beamed ceilings in the lobby and in the six first-floor rooms. Most have pleasant if functional decor, and all have satellite TV. The Pompidou Center and the Picasso Museum are five minutes away. *11 rue du Temple, 75004, tel. 01–42–72–72–22, fax 01–42–72–03–53. 39 rooms. Air-conditioning, in-room data ports, in-room safes, no-smoking rooms. AE, DC, MC, V. Métro: Hôtel de Ville.*

\$\$ Bretonnerie. This small hotel is in a 17th-century *hôtel particulier* (town house) on a tiny street in the Marais, a few minutes' walk from the Pompidou Center. Rooms are done in Louis XIII style, complete with upholstered walls; they vary considerably in size from spacious to cramped. *22 rue Ste-Croix-de-la-Bretonnerie, 75004, tel. 01–48–87–77–63, fax 01–42–77–26–78. 27 rooms, 3 suites. In-room safes. MC, V. Métro: Hôtel de Ville.*

\$\$ Caron de Beaumarchais. The theme of this intimate jewel is the
★ work of Caron de Beaumarchais, who wrote *The Marriage of Figaro* in 1778. Rooms faithfully reflect the taste of 18th-century French nobility. The second- and fifth-floor rooms with balconies are the largest; those on the sixth floor have beguiling views across Right Bank rooftops. *12 rue Vieille-du-Temple, 75004, tel. 01–42–72–34–12, fax 01–42–72–34–63. 19 rooms. Air-conditioning, in-room safes, laundry service. AE, DC, MC, V. Métro: Hôtel de Ville.*

\$\$ Deux-Iles. This converted 17th-century mansion on the Ile St-Louis has long won plaudits for charm and comfort. The delightfully old-fashioned rooms, blessed with exposed beams, are small but airy; ask for one overlooking the little garden courtyard. In winter a roaring fire warms the lounge. *59 rue St-Louis-en-l'Ile, 75004, tel. 01–43–26–13–35, fax 01–43–29–60–25. 17 rooms. Air-conditioning, in-room safes, baby-sitting. AE, MC, V. Métro: Pont-Marie.*

\$–\$\$ Hôtel du 7ᵉ Art. The theme of this hip Marais hotel ("Seventh Art" is what the French call filmmaking) is Hollywood from the '40s to the '6os. Rooms are small and spartan but clean, quiet, and equipped with cable TV. There's no elevator, but there is a pleasant bar. The clientele is young, trendy, and primarily American. *20 rue St-Paul, 75004, tel. 01–44–54–85–00, fax 01–42–77–69–10. 23 rooms. Bar, in-room safes. AE, DC, MC, V. Métro: St-Paul.*

$ Castex. This Marais hotel in a Revolution-era building is a bargain hunter's dream. Rooms are low on frills but squeaky clean and up to date, the owners are extremely friendly, and the prices are rock bottom, which ensures the hotel is often booked months ahead. There's no elevator, and the only TV is in the ground-floor salon. *5 rue Castex, 75004, tel. 01–42–72–31–52, fax 01–42–72–57–91. 29 rooms, 23 with shower. MC, V. Métro: Bastille.*

$ Place des Vosges. A loyal, eclectic clientele swears by this small, historic Marais hotel on a delightful street just off place des Vosges. The Louis XIII–style reception area and rooms with oak-beamed ceilings, rough-hewn stone, and a mix of rustic finds from secondhand shops evoke old Marais. *12 rue de Birague, 75004, tel. 01–42–72–60–46, fax 01–42–72–02–64. 16 rooms. Breakfast room. AE, DC, MC, V. Métro: Bastille.*

5ᵉ Arrondissement (Latin Quarter)

$$$ Jardin du Luxembourg. Blessed with a charming staff and a stylish look, this hotel is one of the most sought after in the Latin Quarter. Rooms are a bit small (common for this neighborhood) but intelligently furnished for optimal space and warmly decorated in ocher, rust, and indigo à la Provençal. Ask for one with a balcony overlooking the street; the best, No. 25, has a peekaboo view of the Eiffel Tower. *5 impasse Royer-Collard, 75005, tel. 01–40–46–08–88, fax 01–40–46–02–28. 27 rooms. Air-conditioning, in-room safes, no-smoking rooms, sauna. AE, DC, MC, V. Métro: Luxembourg.*

$$ Esméralda. Once any *Vogue* editor's best-kept secret, this place
★ used to be the ultimate Left Bank *hôtel de charme*. Set in a fusty 17th-century building across from Notre-Dame, it has long been

cherished for its quirky, cozy, eccentric charm. Some closet-size rooms are nearly overpowered by gaudy imitation antiques or 1970s fabrics, while others could be cleaner. The tiny lobby—adorned with silk flowers, daub and wood moldings, and snoozing cats—is right out of a Flaubert novel. *4 rue St-Julien-le-Pauvre, 75005, tel. 01–43–54–19–20, fax 01–40–51–00–68. 15 rooms with bath, 4 without. No credit cards. Métro: St-Michel.*

$ Grandes Écoles. ★ **Familia.** The hospitable Gaucheron family, the owners, bends over backward for you. About half the rooms feature romantic sepia frescoes of celebrated Paris scenes; others are appointed with exquisite Louis XV–style furnishings or have nice mahogany pieces. Book a month ahead for one with a walk-out balcony on the second or fifth floor. *11 rue des Écoles, 75005, tel. 01–43–54–55–27, fax 01–43–29–61–77. 30 rooms. AE, MC, V. Métro: Cardinal Lemoine.*

$ Grandes Écoles. This delightfully intimate place looks and feels like a country cottage dropped smack in the middle of the Latin Quarter. It's off the street and occupies three buildings on a beautiful leafy garden. Parquet floors, Louis-Philippe furnishings, lace bedspreads, and the absence of TV all add to the rustic ambience. *75 rue du Cardinal Lemoine, 75005, tel. 01–43–26–79–23, fax 01–43–25–28–15. 51 rooms. Parking (fee). MC, V. Métro: Cardinal Lemoine.*

$ Minerve. ★ Fans of the Gaucheron family—and they are legion—will be delighted to learn that the Minerve is now part of the Familia (see *above*) fold. Just next door to the Familia, and twice as big, the hotel has been completely refurbished in the inimitable Gaucheron style: flowers and breakfast tables on the balconies, frescoes in the spacious lobby, tapestries on the walls and cherry-wood furniture in the rooms. It's less intimate than the Familia —but just as charming. *13 rue des Écoles, 75005, tel. 01–43–26–26–04, fax 01–44–07–01–96. 54 rooms. In-room data ports, breakfast room. AE, MC, V. Métro: Cardinal Lemoine.*

6e Arrondissement
(St-Germain/Montparnasse)

$$$$ Relais Christine. On a quiet street between the Seine and
boulevard St-Germain, this luxurious and popular hotel, occupying
16th-century abbey cloisters, oozes romantic ambience. Rooms
are spacious (particularly the duplexes on the upper floors) and
well appointed in old Parisian style; the best have exposed beams
and overlook the garden. *3 rue Christine, 75006, tel. 01–40–51–60–
80; 800/447–7462 in the U.S., fax 01–40–51–60–81. 31 rooms, 18
suites. Bar, air-conditioning, no-smoking rooms, room service, baby-
sitting, laundry service, meeting rooms, parking (free). AE, DC, MC, V. Métro:
Odéon.*

$$$$ Relais St-Germain. The interior-designer owners of this
★ outstanding hotel have exquisite taste and a superb respect for
tradition and detail. Moreover, the rooms are at least twice the
size of those in other hotels in the area for the same price. Much
of the furniture was selected with a knowledgeable eye from the
city's *brocantes* (secondhand dealers), and every room has unique
treasures. Breakfast is included. *9 carrefour de l'Odéon, 75006, tel.
01–43–29–12–05, fax 01–46–33–45–30. 21 rooms, 1 suite. AE, DC, MC,
V. Métro: Odéon.*

$$$–$$$$ Hôtel d'Aubusson. This good-value hotel keeps prices in check
★ while offering original Aubusson tapestries, Versailles-style parquet
floors, a chiseled stone fireplace, and restored antiques. Even the
smallest rooms are a good size by Paris standards, and all are
decked out in rich burgundies, greens, or blues. The 10 best
rooms have canopied beds and ceiling beams. *33 rue Dauphine,
75006, tel. 01–43–29–43–43, fax 01–43–29–12–62. 49 rooms. Bar,
air-conditioning, in-room safes, baby-sitting, laundry service. AE, MC, V.
Métro: Odéon.*

$$$ Hôtel de L'Abbaye. This delightful hotel near St-Sulpice was
transformed from an erstwhile convent. The blend of stylishly
rustic antiques and earthy apricot and ocher tones makes for a

calm, cozy atmosphere. The first-floor rooms open onto the garden; most of those on the upper floors have oak beams and sitting alcoves. The four duplexes with private terraces are more expensive. Breakfast is included. *10 rue Cassette, 75006, tel. 01–45–44–38–11, fax 01–45–48–07–86. 42 rooms, 4 suites. Bar, air-conditioning, room service, baby-sitting, laundry service. AE, MC, V. Métro: St-Sulpice.*

$$ Atelier Montparnasse. This Art Deco–inspired gem of a hotel was designed with style and comfort in mind. Rooms are tastefully decorated and spacious, and all the bathrooms feature mosaic reproductions of famous French paintings. One of the rooms sleeps three. The hotel is within walking distance of the Luxembourg Garden and St-Germain-des-Prés. *49 rue Vavin, 75006, tel. 01–46–33–60–00, fax 01–40–51–04–21. 17 rooms. Bar, room service, baby-sitting, laundry service. AE, DC, MC, V. Métro: Vavin.*

$$ Bonaparte. The congenial staff only makes staying in this intimate place more of a treat. Old-fashioned upholsteries, 19th-century furnishings, and paintings create a quaint feel in the relatively spacious rooms. And the location in the heart of St-Germain is nothing short of fabulous. *61 rue Bonaparte, 75006, tel. 01–43–26–97–37, fax 01–46–33–57–67. 29 rooms. Air-conditioning, in-room safes, refrigerators, laundry service. MC, V. Métro: St-Germain-des-Prés.*

7ᵉ Arrondissement (Invalides/École Militaire)

$$$$ Montalembert. This place is one of Paris's most originally voguish boutique hotels. Whether appointed with traditional or contemporary furnishings, rooms are all about simple lines and chic luxury. Ask about special packages if you're staying for more than three nights. *3 rue de Montalembert, 75007, tel. 01–45–49–68–68; 800/628–8929 in the U.S., fax 01–45–49–69–49. 50 rooms, 6 suites. Restaurant, bar, air-conditioning, in-room data ports, in-room safes, in-room VCRs, room service, baby-sitting, meeting rooms. AE, DC, MC, V. Métro: Rue du Bac.*

\$\$–\$\$\$ **Le Tourville.** Here is a rare find: an intimate, upscale hotel at an
★ affordable price. Each room has crisp, virgin-white damask
upholstery set against pastel or ocher walls, a smattering of
antiques, original artwork, and fabulous old mirrors. The staff
couldn't be more helpful. *16 av. de Tourville, 75007, tel. 01–47–05–
62–62; 800/528–3549 in the U.S., fax 01–47–05–43–90. 27 rooms,
3 junior suites. Bar, breakfast room, air-conditioning, laundry service. AE,
DC, MC, V. Métro: École Militaire. www.hoteltourville.com*

\$\$ **Latour Maubourg.** In the residential heart of the ritzy seventh, a
stone's throw from Invalides, this hotel with a friendly staff has
been inked into many a traveler's journal. Decor is homey and
unpretentious, and with just 10 rooms, the accent is on intimacy
and personalized service. *150 rue de Grenelle, 75007, tel. 01–47–05–
16–16, fax 01–47–05–16–14. 9 rooms, 1 suite. In-room safes. MC, V. Métro:
Latour Maubourg. www.latour-maubourg.fr*

8ᵉ Arrondissement (Champs-Élysées)

\$\$\$\$ **L'Astor.** Following a top-to-bottom makeover by the Westin-
Demeure group, L'Astor has been reborn as a bastion of highly
stylized, civilized chic, thanks to the Sofitel chain. The lobby is Art
Deco; rooms are testimonials to the sober Regency style, with
weighty marble fireplaces and mahogany furnishings. The hotel's
restaurant is supervised by the celebrated chef Joël Robuchon.
*11 rue d'Astorg, 75008, tel. 01–53–05–05–05; 800/937–8461 in the
U.S., fax 01–53–05–05–30. 134 rooms, 5 suites. Restaurant, bar, air-
conditioning, in-room data ports, in-room safes, no-smoking rooms, room
service, massage, health club, baby-sitting, laundry service. AE, DC, MC,
V. Métro: Miromesnil, St-Augustin. www.hotel-astor.net*

\$\$\$\$ **Hôtel Crillon.** Home away from home for movie stars and off-duty
★ celebrities, this is one of Paris's most famous palace hotels. The
Crillon is in two 18th-century town houses on place de la Concorde.
Rooms are lavish, with Rococo and Directoire furnishings and
crystal and gilt wall sconces. The sheer quantity of marble

downstairs—especially in Les Ambassadeurs restaurant—is staggering. *10 pl. de la Concorde, 75008, tel. 01–44–71–15–00; 800/888–4747 in the U.S., fax 01–44–71–15–02. 115 rooms, 45 suites. 2 restaurants, 2 bars, tea shop, air-conditioning, in-room safes, in-room data ports, no-smoking rooms, room service, exercise room, baby-sitting, laundry service, meeting rooms. AE, DC, MC, V. Métro: Concorde. www.crillon-paris.com*

$$$$ George V. Two years and $125 million in renovations later, the George V has finally reopened its glittering gold doors. General Eisenhower's headquarters during the liberation of Paris is now owned by a Saudi prince (who gets first dibs on the $8,500 a night Royal Suite) and managed by the Four Seasons group. The original Art Deco detailings and 17th century tapestries have been restored, the bas-reliefs releafed in gold, and the marble-floor mosaics rebuilt stone by stone. New additions include private health club facilities and the super-luxe Le V restaurant. *31 av. George V, 75008, tel. 01–49–52–70–00, fax 01–49–52–70–10. 184 rooms and 61 suites. Restaurant, bar, air-conditioning, in-room safes, in-room data ports, no-smoking rooms, indoor swimming pool, beauty salons, saunas, health club, business center, meeting rooms. AE, DC, MC, V. Métro: George V. www.fourseasons.com*

$$$$ Hyatt Regency Paris–Madeleine. This stunning Haussmann-esque building near the Opéra Garnier feels more like a boutique hotel than an international business chain, thanks to stylized details like cherry paneling and mismatched bedside tables. Book a room on the seventh or eighth floor facing boulevard Malesherbes for a view of the Eiffel Tower. *24 bd. Malesherbes, 75008, tel. 01–55–27–12–34; 800/223–1234 in the U.S., fax 01–55–27–12–35. 81 rooms, 5 suites. Restaurant, bar, air-conditioning, in-room data ports, in-room safes, no-smoking floors, room service, sauna, exercise room, laundry service, meeting rooms. AE, DC, MC, V. Métro: St-Augustin.*

$$$$ **Lancaster.** The Lancaster—one of Paris's most venerable
★ institutions, now owned by the Savoy group—has been
meticulously transformed into one of the city's most modish
luxury hotels. The clubby decor seamlessly blends the traditional
with the contemporary to evoke an overall feeling of timeless
elegance. *7 rue de Berri, 75008, tel. 01–40–76–40–76; 877/75–PARIS
in the U.S., fax 01–40–76–40–00. 50 rooms, 10 suites. Restaurant, bar,
air-conditioning, in-room data ports, in-room safes, in-room VCRs, room
service, sauna, exercise room, baby-sitting, laundry service, meeting
rooms, parking (fee). AE, DC, MC, V. Métro: George-V.*

9ᵉ Arrondissement (Opéra)

$$$$ **Grand Hôtel Inter-Continental.** Open since 1862, Paris's biggest
luxury hotel has a facade that seems as long as the Louvre. The
grand salon's Art Deco dome and the restaurant's painted ceilings
are registered landmarks. The Art Deco rooms are spacious and
light (ask for one on the top floors). Its famed Café de la Paix is
one of the city's great people-watching spots. *2 rue Scribe, 75009,
tel. 01–40–07–32–32; 800/327–0200 in the U.S., fax 01–42–66–12–
51. 475 rooms, 39 suites. 3 restaurants, 2 bars, air-conditioning, in-
room data ports, in-room safes, in-room VCRs, no-smoking rooms, room
service, sauna, health club, laundry service, business services, meeting rooms.
AE, DC, MC, V. Métro: Opéra.*

12ᵉ Arrondissement (Bastille/Gare de Lyon)

$$–$$$ **Le Pavillon Bastille.** The transformation of this 19th-century *hôtel
particulier* (across from the Opéra Bastille) into a mod, colorful,
high-design hotel garnered architectural awards and a fiercely loyal,
hip clientele. *65 rue de Lyon, 75012, tel. 01–43–43–65–65; 800/
233–2552 in the U.S., fax 01–43–43–96–52. 24 rooms, 1 suite. Bar, air-
conditioning, in-room safes, minibars, room service. AE, DC, MC, V. Métro:
Bastille.*

14ᵉ Arrondissement (Montparnasse)

$$ **Raspail-Montparnasse.** Rooms in this hotel are named after the artists who made Montparnasse the art capital of the world in the '20s and '30s. All are decorated in pastels and contemporary blond-wood furniture. Most are at the low end of this price category; five have spectacular panoramic views of Montparnasse and the Eiffel Tower. *203 bd. Raspail, 75014, tel. 01–43–20–62–86, fax 01–43–20–50–79. 38 rooms. Bar, air-conditioning, in-room safes, meeting rooms. AE, DC, MC, V. Métro: Vavin. www.globe-market.com./h75014raspail.htm*

$ **Parc Montsouris.** This modest hotel in a 1930s villa is on a quiet residential street next to the lovely Parc Montsouris. Attractive oak pieces and high-quality French fabrics embellish the small but clean rooms; satellite TV is another plus. Those with shower are very inexpensive; suites sleep four. *4 rue du Parc-Montsouris, 75014, tel. 01–45–89–09–72, fax 01–45–80–92–72. 28 rooms, 7 suites. Air-conditioning, no-smoking rooms, laundry service. AE, MC, V. Métro: Montparnasse-Bienvenue.*

16ᵉ Arrondissement (Arc de Triomphe/Le Bois)

$$$$ **Saint James Paris.** Touted as the "only château-hôtel" in Paris, this gracious late-19th-century Neoclassical mansion is surrounded by a lush private park. The lavish Art Deco interior was created by designer Andrée Putman. Ten rooms on the third floor open onto a winter garden. The restaurant is reserved for guests; in warm weather meals are served in the garden. *43 av. Bugeaud, 75016, tel. 01–44–05–81–81; 800/447–7462 in the U.S., fax 01–44–05–81–82. 24 rooms, 24 suites. Restaurant, bar, air-conditioning, in-room data ports, in-room safes, no-smoking rooms, room service, sauna, health club, baby-sitting, laundry service, meeting rooms, parking (free). AE, DC, MC, V. Métro: Porte Dauphine.*

$ **Queen's Hôtel.** One of only a handful of hotels in the tony residential district near the Bois de Boulogne, Queen's is a small, comfortable hotel with a high standard of service. Each room focuses on a different 20th-century French artist. The rooms with baths have Jacuzzis. *4 rue Bastien-Lepage, 75016, tel. 01–42–88–89–85, fax 01–40–50–67–52. 21 rooms. Air-conditioning, in-room safes, minibars, no-smoking rooms. AE, DC, MC, V. Métro: Michel-Ange–Auteuil. www.queens-hotel.fr*

17ᵉ Arrondissement (Monceau/Clichy)

$$ **Étoile-Péreire.** Behind a quiet, leafy courtyard in this chic residential district is this unique, intimate hotel, consisting of two parts: a fin-de-siècle building on the street and a 1920s annex overlooking an interior courtyard. Rooms and duplexes are done in deep shades of rose or blue with crisp, white damask upholstery; only suites have air-conditioning. *146 bd. Péreire, 75017, tel. 01–42–67–60–00, fax 01–42–67–02–90. 21 rooms, 5 duplex suites. Bar, in-room safes, no-smoking rooms, laundry service. AE, DC, MC, V. Métro: Péreire.*

PRACTICAL INFORMATION

Revised and updated by Nicola Keegan

Addresses

Addresses in Paris are fairly straightforward: there is the number, the street name and, often, the location in one of Paris's 20 arrondissements (districts): for instance, Paris 75010 or, simply, the last two digits, 10^e, both of which indicate that the address is in the 10th. Due to its large size, the 16th arrondissement has two numbers assigned to it: 75016 and 75116. For the layout of Paris's arrondissements, consult the map at the beginning of the book. They are laid out in a spiral, beginning from the area around the Louvre (1er arrondissement), then moving clockwise out from the city center to the outskirts until it reaches Menilmontant/Père Lachaise (20e arrondissement).

Air Travel to and from Paris

Flying time to Paris is 7 hours from New York, 9½ hours from Chicago, and 11 hours from Los Angeles. Flying time from the United Kingdom to Paris is 1½ hours.

CARRIERS

➤ MAJOR AIRLINES: **Air Canada** (tel. 800/776–3000 in the U.S. and Canada). **Air France** (tel. 800/237–2747 in the U.S.; 08–02–80–28–02 in France). **American Airlines** (tel. 800/433–7300 in the U.S.; 01–69–32–73–07 in France). **British Airways** (tel. 800/247–9297 in the U.S.; 0345/222111 in the U.K.; 08–25–82–54–00 in France). **Continental** (tel. 800/231–0856 in the U.S.; 01–42–99–09–09 in France). **Delta** (tel. 800/241–4141 in the U.S.; 01–47–68–92–92 in France). **Northwest** (tel. 800/225–2525 in the U.S.; 01–42–66–90–00 in France). **Qantas** (tel. 800/227–4500 in the U.S.; 08–03–84–68–46 in France). **TWA** (tel. 800/892–4141 in the U.S.; 08–01–89–28–92 in France). **United** (tel. 800/538–2929 in the U.S.; 08–01–72–72–72 in France). **US Airways** (tel. 800/428–4322 in the U.S.; 01–49–10–29–00 in France).

➤ TRAVEL BETWEEN THE U.K. AND FRANCE: **Air France** (tel. 020/8742–6600 in the U.K.; 08–02–80–28–02 in France). **Air U.K.** (tel. 020/8742–6600 in the U.K.; 08–02–80–28–02 in France; 0345/666–777 in the U.K.; 01–44–56–18–08 in France). **British Airways** (tel. 0345/222–111 in the U.K.; 08–02–80–29–02 in France). **British Midland** (tel. 020/8754–7321; 0345/554–554 in the U.K.; 01–48–62–55–65 in France).

Airports & Transfers

The major airports are Charles de Gaulle (also known as Roissy), 26 km (16 mi) northeast of Paris, and Orly, 16 km (10 mi) south of Paris. It doesn't really matter which one you fly into; both are easily accessible to Paris, though Roissy is the only one with a TGV station.

➤ AIRPORT INFORMATION: **Charles de Gaulle/Roissy** (tel. 01–48–62–22–80 in English). **Orly** (tel. 01–49–75–15–15).

AIRPORT TRANSFERS

From the Charles de Gaulle airport into Paris, your least expensive option is to **take the RER-B line, the suburban express train,** which leaves from beneath Terminal 2 (look for signs for the RER in the airport terminal; you may have to catch the free bus to get to the RER station, which is only a short ride away). Trains to central Paris (Les Halles, St-Michel, Luxembourg) depart every 15 minutes. The fare (including métro connection) is 49 francs, and journey time is about 35 minutes. Note that you have to carry your luggage down to the train tracks, and trains can be crowded if you are traveling during rush hour.

Another way to get into Paris is to **take the Air France bus** between Charles de Gaulle airport and the city (you needn't have flown Air France to use this service). Buses run every 12–20 minutes between the airport and Montparnasse, as well as between the airport and the Arc de Triomphe, with a stop at the Air France air terminal at Porte Maillot. The fare is 60 francs, and journey time is about 40 minutes. Another option is to **take Roissybus, operated by the Paris Transit Authority,** which runs between Charles de Gaulle and the Opéra every 15 minutes; the cost is 48 francs. Note that you have to hail the bus that you want—it will not stop automatically—and that rush-hour traffic can make the trip slow.

At the airport, **taxis are readily available.** Journey time is around 30 minutes, depending on the traffic, and the average fare is 170–300 francs; ask what the fare will be before getting in the taxi. Expect to pay a 6 franc supplement per piece of luggage. Another option is to **arrange a ride with Paris Airports Service or Airport Shuttle,** which can meet you on arrival in a private car and drive you to your destination (about 120 francs for one person, and 89 francs per additional person).

From the Orly airport, the most economical way to get into Paris is to **take the RER-C or Orlyrail line;** catch the free shuttle bus from the terminal to the train station. Trains to Paris leave every 15 minutes. The fare is 30 francs, and journey time is about 35 minutes. Another option is to **take the monorail service, Orlyval,** which runs between the Antony RER-B station and Orly airport every 7 minutes. The fare to downtown Paris is 57 francs.

You can also **take an Air France bus** from Orly to Les Invalides on the Left Bank and Montparnasse; these run every 12 minutes (you need not have flown on Air France to use this service). The fare is 45 francs, and journey time is between 30 and 45 minutes, depending on traffic. Another option is to **take the Paris Transit Authority's Orlybus**; buses leave every 15 minutes for the Denfert-Rochereau métro station; the cost is 30 francs.

In light traffic, taxis take around 25 minutes from Orly to downtown Paris; the fare will be from 100 to 170 francs. Be sure to ask about the fare before getting in the taxi. With advance reservations, Paris Airports Service or Airport Shuttle can pick you up at Orly and drive you directly to your destination. If possible make your Airport Shuttle reservations two to three days in advance; MasterCard and Visa are accepted and the operators speak English. Prices depend on the total number of people traveling.

➤ TAXIS & SHUTTLES: **Air France Bus** (tel. 01–41–56–89–00 for recorded information in English). **Airport Shuttle** (tel. 01–45–38–55–72; 888/426–2705 toll free from the U.S.). **Paris Airports Service** (tel. 01–49–62–78–78).

Bus Travel in Paris

Although it's slower than the métro, traveling by bus is a convenient and scenic way to get around the city. Paris buses are green and white; route number and destination are marked in front and major stopping-places along the sides. The brown bus shelters, topped by red and yellow circular signs, contain timetables and route maps; note that buses must be hailed at these larger bus shelters, as they service multiple lines and routes. Smaller stops are designated simply by a pole with bus numbers.

More than two hundred bus routes run throughout Paris, reaching virtually every nook and cranny of the city. During weekdays and Saturday, buses run every five minutes (as opposed to the 15- to 20-minute wait on Sunday and national holidays). One ticket will take you anywhere within the city; if you get off at any point, your ticket is no longer viable.

A map of the bus system is on the flip side of every métro map, in all métro stations, and at all bus stops. Maps are also located in each bus. A recorded message announces the name of the next stop. To get off, press the red button located on all of the silver poles that run the length of the bus and the *arrêt demandé* light directly behind the driver will light up. Use the rear door to exit.

The Balabus, a public orange-and-white colored bus that runs between May and September, gives an interesting 50-minute tour around the major sights. You can use your Paris Visite, Carte Orange, or Mobilis passes (☞ Métro, *below*), or one to three bus tickets depending on how far you ride. The route runs from La Défense to Gare de Lyon.

➤ **BUS INFORMATION: SNCF** (88 rue St-Lazare, 75009 Paris, tel. 08–36–35–35–39 in English).

FARES & SCHEDULES

Regular buses accept métro tickets, or you can buy a single ticket on board (exact change appreciated) for 8 francs. Most routes operate from 7 AM to 8:30 PM (or 20H30 to the French); some continue to midnight. After 8:30 you must either take the métro or one of the 18 "Noctambus" lines (which are indicated by a brown owl symbol at bus stops). These bus lines operate hourly (1:30–5:30 AM) between Châtelet and various nearby suburbs; they can be stopped by hailing them at any point on their route. Paris-Visite/Mobilis passes work on the Noctambus. A regular ticket costs costs 15 francs.

Business Hours

On weekdays, banks are open generally 9:30 AM–4:30 or 5 PM (note that the Banque de France closes at 3:30), and some banks are also open on Saturday 9–5 as well. Most museums close one day a week—usually either Monday or Tuesday—and on national holidays. Generally, museums and national monuments are open from 10 AM to 5 or 6 PM. A few close for lunch (noon–2) and are open Sunday only in the afternoon. Many of the large museums have one *nocturne* (nighttime) opening per week when they are open until 9:30 or 10 PM. Generally, large shops are open from 9:30 or 10 AM to 6 or 7 PM and don't close at lunchtime. Many of the large department stores stay open until 10 PM on Wednesday or Thursday. Smaller shops and many supermarkets often open earlier (8 AM) but take a lengthy lunch break (1 PM–3 PM) and generally close around 8 PM; small food shops are often open Sunday mornings, 9 AM–1 PM. Most shops close all day Sunday, except some around the Marais, the Bastille, the Latin Quarter, and the Ile de la Cité.

Car Rental

Note that driving in Paris is best avoided, and parking is very difficult to find. You're better off renting a car only when you want to make excursions out of the city. Rates in Paris begin at approximately $70 a day and $200 a week for an economy car with air-conditioning, manual transmission, and unlimited mileage. This does not include tax on car rentals, which is 20.6% or, if you pick it up at the airport, the airport tax. To save money, make reservations before you go.

➤ MAJOR AGENCIES: **Alamo** (tel. 800/522–9696; 020/8759–6200 in the U.K.). **Avis** (tel. 800/331–1084; 800/331–1084 in Canada; 02/9353–9000 in Australia; 09/525–1982 in NewZealand). **Budget** (tel. 800/527–0700; 0870/607–5000 in the U.K., through affiliate Europcar). **Dollar** (tel. 800/800–6000; 0124/622–0111 in the U.K., through affiliate Sixt Kenning; 02/9223–1444 in Australia). **Hertz** (tel. 800/654–3001; 800/263–0600 in Canada;020/8897–2072 in the U.K.; 02/9669–2444 in Australia; 09/256–8690 in New Zealand). **National Car Rental** (tel. 800/227–7368; 020/8680–4800 in the U.K., where it is known as National Europe).

Car Travel

BASIC RULES

In France, you drive on the right and **yield to drivers coming from streets to the right.** However, this rule does not necessarily apply at roundabouts, where you should watch out for just about everyone. You must **wear your seat belt,** and children under 12 may not travel in the front seat. In France **your own driver's license is acceptable.** You must be 18 years old to drive. To rent a car you must be 21 or older and have a major credit card, though you are charged a 110 franc per day supplement if you're under 25.

EMERGENCY SERVICES

If your car breaks down on an expressway, **go to a roadside emergency telephone.** If you have a breakdown anywhere else, find the nearest garage or contact the police.

➤ CONTACTS: **Police** (tel. 17). **Club Automobile de l'Ile de France** (tel. 01–40–55–43–00) is for members only.

PARKING

Finding parking in Paris is very difficult. Meters and ticket machines (pay and display) are common: make sure you **have a supply of 1-, 2-, 5-, and 10-franc coins.** If you're planning on spending a lot of time in Paris with a car, **buy a parking card** (*carte de stationnement*) for 100 francs at any café sporting the red TABAC sign. This card works like a credit card in the parking meters, allowing you to avoid the inconvenience of finding exact change. After depositing enough money (or using your parking card) in the ticket machine, you will receive a receipt; **be sure to display the receipt inside your vehicle,** the dashboard on the passenger side being best. Note that in August, parking is free in certain residential areas; however, only parking meters with a dense yellow circle on them indicate free parking in August; if you do not see the circle, pay.

Customs & Duties

When shopping, **keep receipts** for all purchases. Upon reentering the country, **be ready to show customs officials what you've bought.** If you feel a duty is incorrect or object to the way your clearance was handled, note the inspector's badge number and ask to see a supervisor. If the problem isn't resolved, write to the appropriate authorities, beginning with the port director at your point of entry.

IN CANADA

Canadian residents who have been out of Canada for at least 7 days may bring home C$500 worth of goods duty-free. If you've been away less than 7 days but more than 48 hours, the duty-free allowance drops to C$200; if your trip lasts 24–48 hours, the allowance is C$50. You may not pool allowances with family members. Goods claimed under the C$500 exemption may follow you by mail; those claimed under the lesser exemptions must accompany you. Alcohol and tobacco products may be included in the 7-day and 48-hour exemptions but not in the 24-hour exemption. If you meet the age requirements of the province or territory through which you reenter Canada, you may bring in, duty-free, 1.14 liters (40 imperial ounces) of wine or liquor or 24 12-ounce cans or bottles of beer or ale. If you are 16 or older you may bring in, duty-free, 200 cigarettes and 50 cigars. Check ahead of time with Revenue Canada or the Department of Agriculture for policies regarding meat products, seeds, plants, and fruits.

You may send an unlimited number of gifts worth up to C$60 each duty-free to Canada. Label the package UNSOLICITED GIFT—VALUE UNDER $60. Alcohol and tobacco are excluded.

➤ INFORMATION: **Revenue Canada** (2265 St. Laurent Blvd. S, Ottawa, Ontario K1G 4K3, tel. 613/993–0534; 800/461–9999 in Canada, fax 613/957–8911, www.ccra-adrc.gc.ca).

IN FRANCE
If you're coming from outside the European Union (EU), you may import duty free: (1) 200 cigarettes or 100 cigarillos or 50 cigars or 250 grams of tobacco (twice that if you live outside Europe); (2) 2 liters of wine and, in addition, (a) 1 liter of alcohol over 22% volume (most spirits) or (b) 2 liters of alcohol under 22% volume (fortified or sparkling wine) or (c) 2 more liters of table wine; (3) 50 milliliters of perfume and 250 milliliters of toilet water; (4) 200 grams of coffee, 100 grams of tea; and (5) other goods to the value of 300 francs (100 francs for those under 15).

If you're arriving from an EU country, you may be required to declare all goods and prove that anything over the standard limit is for personal consumption. But there is no limit or customs tariff imposed on goods carried within the EU.

Any amount of French or foreign currency may be brought into France, but foreign currencies converted into francs may be reconverted into a foreign currency only up to the equivalent of 5,000 francs.

➤ INFORMATION: **Direction des Douanes** (16 rue Yves Toudic, 10ᵉ, tel. 01–40–40–39–00).

IN THE U.K.

If you are a U.K. resident and your journey was wholly within the European Union (EU), you won't have to pass through customs when you return to the United Kingdom. If you plan to bring back large quantities of alcohol or tobacco, check EU limits beforehand. ➤ INFORMATION: **HM Customs and Excise** (Dorset House, Stamford St., Bromley, Kent BR1 1XX, tel. 020/7202–4227).

IN THE U.S.

U.S. residents who have been out of the country for at least 48 hours (and who have not used the $400 allowance or any part of it in the past 30 days) may bring home $400 worth of foreign goods duty-free.

U.S. residents 21 and older may bring back 1 liter of alcohol duty-free. In addition, regardless of your age, you are allowed 200 cigarettes and 100 non-Cuban cigars. Antiques, which the U.S. Customs Service defines as objects more than 100 years old, enter duty-free, as do original works of art done entirely by hand, including paintings, drawings, and sculptures.

You may also send packages home duty-free: up to $200 worth of goods for personal use, with a limit of one parcel per addressee per day (except alcohol or tobacco products or perfume worth more than $5); label the package PERSONAL USE and attach a list of its contents and their retail value. Do not label the package UNSOLICITED GIFT or your duty-free exemption will drop to $100. Mailed items do not affect your duty-free allowance on your return.

➤ INFORMATION: **U.S. Customs Service** (1300 Pennsylvania Ave. NW, Washington, DC 20229, www.customs.gov; inquiries tel. 202/354–1000; complaints c/o Office of Regulations and Rulings; registration of equipment c/o Resource Management, tel. 202/927–0540).

Discounts & Deals

Paris Tourist Offices, railroad stations, major métro stations, and participating museums sell the *Carte Musées et Monuments* (Museums and Monuments Pass), which offers unlimited access to more than 65 museums and monuments in Paris over a one-, three-, or five- consecutive day period; the cost, respectively, is 80, 160, and 240 francs. Temporary exhibitions are not included in this pass. This pass is beneficial if you are going to visit many museums and monuments in a short amount of time, but if you don't plan on seeing that many museums or monuments, you may be better off paying per sight.

Electricity

To use your U.S.-purchased electric-powered equipment, **bring a converter and adapter.** The electrical current in Paris is 220 volts, 50 cycles alternating current (AC); wall outlets take continental-type plugs, with two round prongs.

If your appliances are dual-voltage, you'll need only an adapter. Don't use 110-volt outlets marked FOR SHAVERS ONLY for high-wattage appliances such as blow-dryers. Most laptops operate equally well on 110 and 220 volts and so require only an adapter.

Embassies

➤ **CANADA:** 35 av. Montaigne, Paris, 8ᵉ, tel. 01–44–43–29–00, métro Franklin-D.-Roosevelt, weekdays 8:30–11.

➤ **UNITED KINGDOM:** 35 rue du Faubourg-St-Honoré, Paris, 8ᵉ, tel. 01–44–51–31–00, métro Madeleine, weekdays 9:30–12:30 and 2:30–5.

➤ **UNITED STATES:** 2 rue St-Florentin, Paris, 1ᵉʳ, tel. 01–43–12–22–22 in English; 01–43–12–23–47 in emergencies, métro Concorde, weekdays 9–3.

Emergencies

Call the **police** (17) if there has been a crime or an act of violence. On the street, some French phrases that may be needed in an emergency are: *Au secours!* (Help!), *urgence* (emergency), *samu* (ambulance), *pompiers* (firemen), *poste de station* (police station), *médicin* (doctor), and *hôpital* (hospital).

➤ **DOCTORS & DENTISTS: SOS Dentists** (tel. 01–43–37–51–00). **SOS Doctors** (tel. 01–47–07–77–77).

➤ **EMERGENCY SERVICES: Ambulance** (tel. 15). **Fire Department** (tel. 18). **Police** (tel. 17). These numbers are toll-free and can be dialed from any phone.

➤ **HOSPITALS: The American Hospital** (63 bd. Victor Hugo, Neuilly, tel. 01–47–47–70–15). **The Hertford British Hospital** (3 rue Barbès, Levallois-Perret, tel. 01–46–39–22–22).

➤ **LATE-NIGHT AND 24-HOUR PHARMACIES: Dhéry** (Galerie des Champs, 84 av. des Champs-Élysées, 8ᵉ, tel. 01–45–62–02–41) is open 24 hours. **Pharmacie des Arts** (106 bd. Montparnasse, 14ᵉ) is open daily until midnight. **Pharmacie Matignon** (rue Jean Mermoz, at the Rond-Point de Champs-Élysées, 8ᵉ) is open daily until 2 AM.

Holidays

In May, there is a holiday nearly every week, so be prepared for stores, banks, and museums to shut their doors for days at a time. If a holiday falls on a Tuesday or Thursday, many businesses *font le pont* (make the bridge) and close on that Monday or Friday as well. Bastille Day (July 14) is observed in true French form. Celebrations begin on the evening of the 13th and finish the next day with an annual military parade.

January 1 (New Year's Day); April 16 (Easter Monday); May 1 (Labor Day); May 8 (VE Day); May 24 (Ascension); June 4 (Pentecost Monday); July 14 (Bastille Day); August 15 (Assumption); November 1 (All Saints); November 11 (Armistice); December 25 (Christmas).

Métro

Métro stations are recognizable either by a large yellow M within a circle or by the distinctive curly green Art Nouveau railings and archway bearing the full title (Métropolitain). Taking the métro is the most efficient way to get around Paris.

Fourteen métro and two RER (Réseau Express Régional, or the Regional Express Network) lines crisscross Paris and the suburbs, and you are seldom more than 500 yards from the nearest station. The métro network connects at several points in Paris with the RER, the commuter trains that go from the city center to the suburbs. RER trains crossing Paris on their way from suburb to suburb can be great time-savers because they only make a few stops in the city (you can use the same tickets for both the métro and the RER within Paris).

It's essential to **know the name of the last station on the line you take,** as this name appears on all signs. A connection (you can make as many as you like on one ticket) is called a *correspondance*. At junction stations, illuminated orange signs bearing the name of the line terminus appear over the correct corridors for each correspondance. Illuminated blue signs marked *sortie* indicate the station exit. Note that tickets are only valid inside the gates or *limites*.

Métro service starts at 5:30 AM and continues until 1:00 AM, when the last train on each line reaches its terminus. Some lines and stations in the less salubrious parts of Paris are a bit risky at night, in particular Lines 2 and 13. But in general, the métro is relatively safe throughout, providing you **don't walk around with your wallet hanging out of your back pocket or (especially women) travel alone late at night.**

FARES & SCHEDULES
All métro tickets and passes are valid not only for the métro, but also for all RER and bus travel within Paris. Métro tickets cost 8 francs each; a *carnet* (10 tickets for 55 francs) is a better value. The best deal is the weekly (*coupon jaune*) or monthly (*carte orange*) ticket, sold according to zone. Zones 1 and 2 cover the entire métro network; tickets cost 82 francs a week or 279 francs a month. If you plan to take suburban trains to visit places in Ile-de-France, consider a four-zone (Versailles, St-Germain-en-Laye; 134 francs a week) or six-zone (Rambouillet, Fontainebleau; 184 francs a week) ticket. For these weekly/monthly tickets, you need a pass (available from rail and major métro stations) and a passport-size photograph (many stations have photo booths).

The advantage of one-day (Mobilis) and three- and five-day (Paris Visite) unlimited travel tickets for the métro, bus, and RER is that, unlike the coupon jaune, which is good from Monday morning to Sunday evening, Mobilis and Paris Visite passes are valid starting any day of the week and also give you discounts on a limited number of museums and tourist attractions. The price is 55 francs (one-day), 90 francs (two-day), 120 francs (three-day), and 175 francs (five-day) for Paris only. Suburbs such as Versailles and St-Germain-en-Laye cost 175 (one-day). Disneyland Paris costs 155, 225, 280, and 350 francs respectively for a one- to four-day pass.

Access to métro and RER platforms is through an automatic ticket barrier. Slide your ticket in and pick it up as it pops out. Be certain to **keep your ticket during your journey;** you'll need it to leave the RER system and in case you run into any green-clad ticket inspectors who will impose a big fine if you can't produce your ticket.

➤ Métro Information: **RATP** (Pl. de la Madeleine, 8ᵉ can; 53 bis quai des Grands-Augustins, 6ᵉ, tel. 08–36–68–41–14, www.ratp.fr); open daily 9–5.

Money Matters

Like many capital cities, Paris is expensive. But if you avoid the obvious tourist traps, you can find more affordable places to eat and shop. Note that in cafés, bars, and some restaurants, it's less expensive to eat or drink standing at the counter than it is to sit at a table. Two prices are listed, *au comptoir* (at the counter) and *à salle* (at a table), and sometimes a third for the terrace. A cup of coffee, standing at a bar, costs from 7 francs; if you sit, it will cost 10–40 francs.

Expect to pay 40–70 francs for a short taxi ride. Museum entry is 20–45 francs, though there are hours or days of the week when admission is reduced or free.

ATMS

Fairly common in Paris, ATMs are one of the easiest ways to get francs. Although ATM transaction fees may be higher abroad than at home, banks usually offer excellent, wholesale exchange rates through ATMs. You may, however, have to look around for Cirrus and Plus locations; it's a good idea to get a list of locations from your bank before you go. Note, too, that you may have better luck with ATMs if you're using a credit card or debit card that is also a Visa or MasterCard, rather than just your bank card.

To get cash at ATMs in Paris, your pin must be four digits long. Note, too, that you may be charged by your bank for using ATMs overseas; inquire at your bank about charges.

CREDIT CARDS

Throughout this guide, the following abbreviations are used: **AE,** American Express; **DC,** Diner's Club; **MC,** Master Card; and **V,** Visa.

➤ REPORTING LOST CARDS: **American Express** (336/939–1111 or 336/668–5309) call collect. **Diner's Club** (303/799–1504) call collect. **Mastercard** (0800/90–1387). **Visa** (0800/90–1179; collect: 410/581–9994).

CURRENCY

Until January 1st, 2002, the French franc (fr) and the centime will remain the main units of currency in France, but after that date, the new single European Union (EU) currency, the euro, will take over. Until then, people will use the franc in their day-to-day transactions and travelers will continue to exchange their money for France's colorful 500-, 200-, 100-, 50-, and 20-franc banknotes, 20-, 10-, 5-, 2-, and 1-franc coins, and tiny 20-, 10-, and 5-centimes coins. At press time (summer 2000), the exchange rate was about 7.30 francs to the U.S. dollar, 4.90 to the Canadian dollar, and 10.00 to the pound sterling. For the euro denomination, the exchange rate was about 1.12 euros to the U.S dollar and 0.74 to the Canadian dollar.

Remaining francs will stay in circulation up to July 1, 2002, the date of the final demise of the franc. In the meantime, the euro is slowly but surely becoming a part of daily European life; for every item purchased the price in both francs and euros has to be, by law, listed to familiarize buyers with this change. Under the euro system, there are eight coins: 1 and 2 euros, plus 1, 2, 5, 10, 20, and 50 centimes, or cents, of the euro. All coins have one side that has the value of the euro on it and the other side with each countries' own unique national symbol. There are seven notes: 5, 10, 20, 50, 100, 200, and 500 euros. Notes are the same for all countries.

CURRENCY EXCHANGE

These days, the easiest way to get francs is through ATMs (☞ *above*). It's a good idea, however, to bring some francs with you from home and to always have some cash and traveler's checks as back up. For the best deal, compare rates at banks (which usually have the most favorable rates) and booths and look for exchange booths that clearly state "no commission." Of all the banks in Paris, Banque de Paris generally has the best rates.

➤ EXCHANGE SERVICES: **International Currency Express** (tel. 888/ 278–6628 for orders, www.foreignmoney.com). **Thomas Cook Currency Services** (tel. 800/287–7362 for telephone orders and retail locations, www.us.thomascook.com).

TRAVELER'S CHECKS

The benefit of traveler's checks is that lost or stolen checks can usually be replaced within 24 hours.

Passports & Visas

All citizens of Canada, the United States, and the United Kingdom, even infants, need only a valid passport to enter France for stays of up to 90 days. If you lose your passport, promptly call the nearest embassy or consulate and the local police.

➤ CANADIAN CITIZENS: **Passport Office** (tel. 819/994–3500 or 800/ 567–6868, www.dfait-maeci.gc.ca/passport).

➤ U.K. CITIZENS: **London Passport Office** (tel. 0990/210–410) for fees and documentation requirements and to request an emergency passport.

➤ U.S. CITIZENS: **National Passport Information Center** (tel. 900/225–5674; calls are 35¢ per minute for automated service, $1.05 per minute for operator service).

Sightseeing Tours

BIKE TOURS

A number of companies organize bike tours around Paris and its environs (Versailles, Chantilly, and Fontainebleau) for about 150–200 francs per person.

➤ INFORMATION: **Butterfield & Robinson** (70 Bond St., Toronto, Canada M5B 1X3, tel. 416/864–1354 or 800/678–1147). **Paris Bike** (83 rue Daguerre, 14ᵉ, tel. 01–45–38–58–58). **Paris à Vélo, C'est Sympa** (37 bd. Bourdon, 4ᵉ, tel. 01–48–87–60–01).

BOAT TOURS

Boat trips along the Seine run throughout the day and evening for a cost of 40–100 francs. Many of the tours include lunch or dinner for an average cost of 300 francs–600 francs. Reservations for meals are usually essential and some require jacket and tie.

Bateaux-Mouches boats depart from the Pont de l'Alma (Right Bank) 10–noon, 2–7, and 8:30–10:30. Lunch is served at 1 PM and dinner at 8:30 PM. Bateaux Parisiens–Tour Eiffel boats depart from the Pont d'Iéna (Left Bank) every half hour in summer and every hour in winter, starting at 10 AM. The last boat leaves at 9 PM (11 PM in summer). There are lunch and dinner cruises. Bat-O-Bus's trip along the Seine without commentary gives you the advantage being able to get on and off at any one of five stops along the river, including Trocadéro, Musée d'Orsay, the Louvre, Notre-Dame, and Hôtel de Ville. Take it one stop for 20 francs, pay 60 francs for a full-day ticket, or buy a season ticket for 250 francs. Note that it operates from April 15 to October 31 and departs every half hour between 10 and 6. Canauxrama organizes leisurely canal tours in flat-bottom barges along the St-Martin and Ourcq canals in East Paris. Departures from the quai de la Loire are at 9:15 and 2:45, and departures from the Bassin de l'Arsenal (opposite 50 boulevard de la Bastille) are at 9:30 and 2:30. The trip lasts about 2¼ hours. Reservations should be made. Paris Canal runs three-hour trips with bilingual commentary between the Musée d'Orsay and the Parc de La Villette, between April and mid-November only. Reservations are essential. Vedettes du Pont Neuf boats depart every half hour from the Square du Vert Galant, 10–noon, 1:30–6:30, and 9–10:30 from March to October. Yachts de Paris organizes 2½-hour "gourmet cruises" (for about 890 francs) year-round.

➤ FEES & SCHEDULES: **Bateaux-Mouches** (Pont de l'Alma, 8ᵉ, tel. 01–42–25–96–10). **Bateaux Parisiens-Tour Eiffel** (Pont d'Iéna, 7ᵉ, tel. 01–44–11–33–44). **Bat-O-Bus** (Pont d'Iéna, 7ᵉ, tel. 01–44–11–33–44 or 01–44–11–33–99). **Canauxrama** (5 bis quai de la Loire, 19ᵉ; Bassin de l'Arsenal, 12ᵉ; tel. 01–42–39–15–00). **Paris Canal** (19 quai de la Loire, 19ᵉ, tel. 01–42–40–96–97). **Vedettes du Pont Neuf** (Ile de la Cité, 1ᵉʳ, tel. 01–46–33–98–38). **Yachts de Paris** (Port de Javel, tel. 01–44–54–14–70).

BUS TOURS
For a two-hour orientation tour by bus, the standard price is about 150 francs. The two largest bus tour operators are Cityrama and Paris Vision; for a more intimate—albeit expensive—tour of the city, Cityrama also runs several minibus excursions per day. Paris Bus gives tours in a London-style double-decker bus. You can catch the bus at any of nine pickup points; tickets cost 125 francs and allow you unlimited use for two days. For 135 francs the "Paris Open Tour" gives you two days of freedom to visit Paris in a double-decker bus with an open top. The bilingual tour lasts about two hours but you can get on and off as you please since the bus stops at over 20 spots along a circular route. A copy of the timetables for these tours are available from the main Paris Tourist Office (☞ Visitor Information, *below*). RATP (Paris Transit Authority) also gives guide-accompanied excursions in and around Paris by bus.

➤ FEES & SCHEDULES: **Air France** (119 av. des Champs-Élysées, 8ᵉ, tel. 01–44–08–22–22). **American Express** (11 rue Scribe, 9ᵉ, tel. 01–47–77–77–07). **Cityrama** (4 Pl. des Pyramides, 1ᵉʳ, tel. 01–44–

55–61–00). **Paris Bus** (tel. 01–42–30–55–50). **Paris Vision** (214 rue de Rivoli, 1er, tel. 01–42–60–31–25). **RATP** (Pl. de la Madeleine, 8e; 53 bis quai des Grands-Augustins, 6^e, tel. 08–36–68–41–14. **Wagons-Lits** (31 rue Coloniel Pierre Avia, 15^e, tel. 01–41–33–68–00).

➤ Fees & Schedules: **Delta Lima** (tel. 01–40–68–01–23).

MINIBUS TOURS

Paris Bus and Paris Major Limousine organizes tours of Paris and environs by luxury minibuses (for 4 to 15 passengers) for a minimum of four hours. The price varies from 1,700 to 2,600 francs. Reservations are essential.

➤ Information: **Paris Bus** (22 rue de la Prevoyance, Vincennes, tel. 01–43–65–55–55). **Paris Major Limousine** (6 pl. de la Madeleine, 8^e, tel. 01–44–52–50–00).

WALKING TOURS

There are a number of English-language walking tours of Paris. Walking tours generally last about two hours and cost about 60 francs. Paris Contact arranges walking tours of popular sights such as the Louvre and Versailles and unique theme tours, such as "Jefferson's Paris" and "The Paris of Proust" and can, upon request, do individually organized tours. Paris Walking Tours offers a wide variety of tours, from neighborhood visits to museum tours and theme tours (such as "Hemingway's Paris"). Bohemian Paris organizes a stroll on the Left Bank, filled with literary discussion, biographical information, and gossipy anecdotes about Paris in the '20s; this tour, led by a university professor and writer, costs 200 francs and lasts two and a half hours. Black Paris Tours organizes a variety of tours exploring the places made famous by African-American musicians, writers, artists, and political exiles. Tours include a four- to five-hour walking-bus-metro tour (350 francs) that offers first-time visitors a city orientation and a primer in the history of African-Americans in Paris. Other options include "Montmartre/Pigalle:

The 1920s Harlem of Paris," and tours of top African and soul food restaurants.

➤ FEES & SCHEDULES: **Bohemian Paris** (tel. 01–56–24–36–00). **Butterfield & Robinson** (70 Bond St., Toronto, Canada M5B 1X3, tel. 416/864–1354 or 800/678–1147). **Paris Contact** (tel. 01–42–51–08–40). **Paris Walking Tours** (tel. 01–48–09–21–40). **Black Paris Tours** (tel. 01–46–37–03–96).

Smoking

The French are smokers—there's no way around it. And they're notorious for disregarding the "Evin" law, which prohibits smoking in public places, with little retribution. Even in restaurants, cafés, and train and métro stations that have no-smoking sections, you'll see people smoking. Your best bet for finding as smoke-free an environment as possible is to stick to the larger cafés and restaurants where there might be more clearly defined smoking and no-smoking areas.

SNCF trains have cars designated for smoking and no-smoking (specify when you make reservations), and these are among the few places where the laws are respected. Some hotels, too, have designated no-smoking rooms; ask for these when reserving.

Taxes

All taxes must be included in affixed prices in France. Prices in **restaurants and hotel prices must by law include taxes and service charges:** if these appear as additional items on your bill, you should complain. VAT (value added tax, known in France as TVA), at a standard rate of 20.6% (33% for luxury goods), is included in the price of many goods, but **foreigners are often entitled to a refund.**

VALUE-ADDED TAX

Global Refund is a V.A.T. refund service that makes getting your moneyback hassle-free. The service is available Europe-wide at 130,000 affiliated stores. In participating stores, **ask for the**

Global Refund form (called a Shopping Cheque). Have it stamped like any customs form by customs officials when you leave the European Union. Then take the form to one of the more than 700 Global Refund counters—conveniently located at every major airport and border crossing—and your money will be refunded on the spot in the form of cash, check, or a refund to your credit-card account (minus a small percentage for processing).

Global Refund (707 Summer St.,Stamford, CT 06901,tel. 800/566–9828, fax 203/674–8709,www.globalrefund.com).

➤ **V.A.T. REFUNDS: Europe Tax-Free Shopping** (233 S. Wacker Dr., Suite 9700, Chicago, IL 60606-6502, tel. 312/382–1101).

Taxis

Taxi rates are based on location and time. Daytime rates, A (7 AM–7 PM), within Paris are 3.53 francs per kilometer, and nighttime rates, B, are around 5.83 francs per kilometer. Suburban zones and airports, C, are 7.16 per kilometer. There is a basic hire charge of 13 francs for all rides, a 6-franc supplement per piece of luggage, and a 5-franc supplement if you're picked up at a SNCF station. Waiting time is charged at 130 francs per hour. The easiest way to get a taxi is to **ask your hotel or a restaurant to call a taxi for you or go to the nearest taxi stand** (you can find one every couple of blocks); cabs with their signs lit can be hailed but are annoyingly difficult to spot. Tip the driver about 10%.

Telephones

AREA & COUNTRY CODES
The country code for France is 33. The first two digits of French numbers are a prefix determined by zone: Paris and Ile-de-France, 01; the northwest, 02; the northeast, 03; the southeast, 04; and the southwest, 05.

Note that **when dialing France from abroad, drop the initial o from the telephone number** (all numbers listed in this book include the initial o, which is used for calling numbers *from within* France). To call a telephone number in Paris from the United States, dial 011–33 plus the phone number minus the initial o (phone numbers in this book are listed with the full 10 digits, which you use to make local calls). To call France from the United Kingdom, dial 00–33, then dial the number in France minus the initial o.

DIRECTORY & OPERATOR ASSISTANCE

To find a number in France, **dial 12 for information.** For international inquiries, dial 00–33 plus the country code.

INTERNATIONAL CALLS

To make a direct international call out of France, dial 00 and wait for the tone, then dial the country code (1 for the United States and Canada, 44 for the United Kingdom) and the area code (minus any initial o) and number.

Expect to be overcharged if you make calls from your hotel. Approximate daytime rates, per minute, are 2.25 francs to the United States and Canada (8:00 AM–9:30 PM), and 2.10 francs for the United Kingdom (2:00 PM–8:00 PM); reduced rates at other time intervals, per minute, are 1.80 francs to the United States and Canada and 1.65 francs to the United Kingdom.

To call home with the help of an operator, dial 00–33 plus the country code. There is an automatic 44.5 franc service charge.

Telephone cards (☞ *below*) are sold that enable you to make long-distance and international calls from pay phones.

LOCAL CALLS

When making a local call in Paris or to Ile-de-France, **dial the full 10-digit number, including the initial o.** A local call costs 74 centimes for every three minutes.

LONG-DISTANCE CALLS

To call from region to region within France, **dial the full 10-digit number, including the initial 0.**

LONG-DISTANCE SERVICES

AT&T, MCI, and Sprint access codes make calling long distance relatively convenient, but you may find the local access number blocked in many hotel rooms. First ask the hotel operator to connect you. If the hotel operator balks, ask for an international operator, or dial the international operator yourself. One way to improve your odds of getting connected to your long-distance carrier is to travel with more than one company's calling card (a hotel may block Sprint, for example, but not MCI). If all else fails, call from a pay phone.

➤ ACCESS CODES: **AT&T Direct** (tel. 08–00–99–00–11; 08–00–99–01–11; 800/222–0300 for information). **MCI WorldPhone** (tel. 08–00–99–00–19; 800/444–4444 for information). **Sprint International Access** (tel. 08–00–99–00–87; 800/793–1153 for information).

PHONE CARDS

Most French pay phones are operated by *télécartes* (phone cards), which you can buy from post offices, tabacs, and métro stations. These phone cards will save you money and hassle, since it's hard to find phones that take change these days. There are two types of cards: the *télécarte international*, which allows you to make local calls and offers greatly reduced rates on international calls (instructions are in English and the cost is 50 francs for 60 units or 100 francs for 120 units); and the simple *télécarte*, which allows you to make calls in France (the cost is 49 francs for 50 units; 97.5 francs for 120 units). You can also use your credit card in much the same way as a télécarte, but it's much more expensive.

In a few cafés you may still be able to find pay phones that operate with 1-, 2-, and 5-franc coins (1.5 francs for local calls).

Lift the receiver, place your coin(s) in the appropriate slots, and dial.

Tipping

Bills in bars and restaurants must, by law, include service, but **it is customary to round out your bill with some small change** unless you're dissatisfied. In expensive restaurants, it's common to leave an additional 5% of the bill on the table.

Tip taxi drivers and hairdressers about 10% of the bill. Give theater and cinema ushers a couple of francs. In some theaters and hotels, cloakroom attendants may expect nothing (watch for signs that say *pourboire interdit*—tipping forbidden); otherwise, give them 5 francs. Washroom attendants usually get 2 francs, though the sum is often posted. If you stay more than two or three days in a hotel, it is customary to leave something for the chambermaid—about 10 francs per day. Expect to pay about 10 francs (5 francs in a moderately priced hotel) to the person who carries your bags or who hails you a taxi. Train and airport porters get a fixed sum (6–10 francs) per bag. Museum guides should get 5–10 francs after a guided tour.

Train Travel to and from Paris

The SNCF, France's rail system, is fast, punctual, comfortable, and comprehensive. There are various options: local trains, overnight trains with sleeping accommodations, and the high-speed TGV, or *Trains à Grande Vitesse*.

Paris has six main rail stations: Gare du Nord (northern France, northern Europe, and England via Calais or Boulogne); Gare St-Lazare (Normandy, England via Dieppe); Gare de l'Est (Strasbourg, Luxembourg, Basel, and central Europe); Gare de Lyon (Lyon, Marseille, the Riviera, Geneva, Italy); Gare d'Austerlitz (Loire Valley, southwest France, Spain); and Gare Montparnasse (southwest France).

FARES, SCHEDULES, & RESERVATIONS

You can **call for train information or reserve tickets in any Paris station,** irrespective of destination. If you know what station you'll depart from, you can get a free schedule there (while supplies last), or you can access the new multilingual computerized schedule information network at any Paris station. You can also make reservations and buy your ticket while at the computer. Go to the Grandes Lignes counter for travel within France and to the Billets Internationaux desk if you're heading out of the country. Note that calling the SNCF's 08 number (☞ *below*) will cost you money (you're charged per minute), so it's better just to go to the nearest station and make reservations.

SEAT RESERVATIONS ARE REQUIRED ON TGVS, and are a good idea on trains that may be crowded—particularly in summer and holidays on popular routes. You also need a reservation for sleeping accommodations.

➤ **TRAIN INFORMATION: BritRail Travel** (tel. 800/677–8585 in the U.S.; 020/7834–2345 in the U.K.). **Eurostar** (tel. 08–36–35–35–39 in France; 0870/518–6186 in the U.K., www.eurostar.com). **InterCity Europe** (Victoria Station, London, tel. 020/7834–2345; 020/7828–0892; 0990/848–848 for credit-card bookings). **Rail Europe** (tel. 800/942–4866 in the U.S., www.raileurope.com). **SNCF** (88 rue St-Lazare, 75009 Paris, tel. 08–36–35–35–35, www.sncf.fr).

BETWEEN THE U.K. AND FRANCE

Short of flying, the "Chunnel" is the fastest way to cross the English Channel: 3 hours from London's central Waterloo Station to Paris's central Gare du Nord, 35 minutes from Folkestone to Calais, and 60 minutes from motorway to motorway. Round-trip tickets range from 3,400 francs for first class to 690 francs for second class. It's a good idea to **make a reservation if you're traveling with your car on a Chunnel train;** cars without reservations, if they can get on at all, are charged 20 percent extra.

British Rail also has four daily departures from London's Victoria Station, all linking with the Dover–Calais/Boulogne ferry services through to Paris. There is also an overnight service on the Newhaven–Dieppe ferry. Journey time is about eight hours. Credit-card bookings are accepted by phone or in person at a British Rail Travel Centre.

➤ CAR TRANSPORT: **Le Shuttle** (tel. 0870/535–3535 in the U.K.; 03–21–00–61–00 in France, www.eurotunnel.co.uk).

➤ PASSENGER SERVICE: **BritRail Travel** (tel. 800/677–8585 in the U.S.; 020/7834–2345 in the U.K.). **Eurostar** (tel. 0870/518–6186 in the U.K.; 08–36–35–35–39 in France, www.eurostar.com). **InterCity Europe** (Victoria Station, London, tel. 020/7834–2345; 020/7828–0892; 0870/584–8848 for credit-card bookings). **Rail Europe** (tel. 800/942–4866 in the U.S., www.raileurope.com).

Visitor Information

FRANCE TOURIST INFORMATION

France On-Call (tel. 410/286–8310 weekdays 9–7, www.francetourism.com). **Chicago** (676 N. Michigan Ave., Chicago, IL 60611). **Los Angeles** (9454 Wilshire Blvd., Suite 715, Beverly Hills, CA 90212). **New York City** (444 Madison Ave., 16th floor, New York, NY 10022). **Canada** (1981 Ave. McGill College, Suite 490, Montréal, Québec H3A 2W9). **U.K.** 178 Piccadilly, London W1V 0AL, tel. 171/6399–3500, fax 171/6493–6594.

LOCAL TOURISM INFORMATION

Espace du Tourisme d'Ile-de-France (Carrousel du Louvre, 99 rue de Rivoli, 75001 tel. 08–03–81–80–00 or 01–44–50–19–98). **Office du Tourisme de la Ville de Paris** (Paris Tourist Office, 127 av. des Champs-Élysées, tel. 01–49–52–53–54; 01–49–52–53–56 for recorded information in English).

Web Sites

Do check out the World Wide Web when you're planning. You'll find everything from current weather forecasts to virtual tours of famous cities. Fodor's Web site, www.fodors.com, is a great place to start your on-line travels. For more specific information on Paris, visit: **Eurostar** (www.eurail.com/ www.eurostar.com). **Louvre Museum** (mistral.culture.fr/louvre/louvrea.htm). **French Embassy** (www.france.diplomatie.fr). **French Government Tourist Office** (www.francetourism.com). **French Ministry of Culture** (www.culture.fr). **Paris Tourist Office** (www.paris.org). **Rail Europe** (www.raileurope.com). **RATP** (www.ratp.fr). **SNCF** (www.sncf.fr).

When to Go

The major tourist season in France stretches from Easter to mid-September, but Paris has much to offer in every season. Paris in the early spring can be disappointingly damp, though it's relatively tourist free; May and June are delightful, with good weather and plenty of cultural and other attractions. July and August can be sultry. If you're undeterred by the hot weather and the pollution, you'll notice a fairly relaxed atmosphere around the city, as this is the month when most Parisians are on vacation. September is ideal. Cultural life revives after the summer break, and sunny weather often continues through the first half of October. The ballet and theater are in full swing in November, but the weather is part wet and cold, part bright and sunny. December is dominated by the *fêtes de fin d'année* (end-of-year festivities), and a busy theater, ballet, and opera season into January.

CLIMATE

The following are the average daily maximum and minimum temperatures for Paris.

Jan.	43F	6C	May	68F	20C	Sept.	70F	21C
	34	1		49	10		53	12
Feb.	45F	7C	June	73F	23C	Oct.	60F	16C
	34	1		55	13		46	8
Mar.	54F	12C	July	76F	25C	Nov.	50F	10C
	39	4		58	14		40	5
Apr.	60F	16C	Aug.	75F	24C	Dec.	44F	7C
	43	6		58	14		36	2

INDEX

FODOR'S POCKET PARIS

EDITORS: Robert I. C. Fisher, Sharron S. Wood

EDITORIAL CONTRIBUTORS: Simon Hewitt, Nicola Keegan, Alexander Lobrano, Christopher Mooney, Ian Phillips, Brandy Whittingham

EDITORIAL PRODUCTION: Tom Holton

MAPS: David Lindroth, *cartographer*; Bob Blake and Rebecca Baer, *map editors*

DESIGN: Fabrizio La Rocca, *creative director*; Tigist Getachew, *art director*

PRODUCTION/MANUFACTURING: Robert B. Shields

COVER PHOTOGRAPH: Catherine Karnow/Corbis

ISBN 0–679–00573–0

ISSN 1094–2998

IMPORTANT TIP

Although all prices, opening times, and other details in this book are based on information supplied to us at press time, changes occur all the time in the travel world, and Fodor's cannot accept responsibility for facts that become outdated or for inadvertent errors or omissions. So **always confirm information when it matters,** especially if you're making a detour to visit a specific place.

SPECIAL SALES

Fodor's Travel Publications are available at special discounts for bulk purchases for sales promotions or premiums. Special editions, including personalized covers, excerpts of existing guides, and corporate imprints, can be created in large quantities for special needs. For more information, contact your local bookseller or write to Special Markets, Fodor's Travel Publications, 280 Park Avenue, New York, NY 10017. Inquiries from Canada should be directed to your local Canadian bookseller or sent to Random House of Canada, Ltd., Marketing Department, 2775 Matheson Boulevard East, Mississauga, Ontario L4W 4P7. Inquiries from the United Kingdom should be sent to Fodor's Travel Publications, 20 Vauxhall Bridge Road, London SW1V 2SA, England.

PRINTED IN THE UNITED STATES OF AMERICA

10 9 8 7 6 5 4 3 2 1